HAND

TO THE

PLOUGH

To
JUDITH, JANICE, STUART,
DEBORAH, ELIZABETH, RICHARD,
CHRISTINE, ANGELA, KATHRYN
my nine wonderful grandchildren, whose
love gives me endless delight, in the hope
and prayer that through trust in Christ
we shall continue to enjoy our 'togetherness'
on earth and in heaven.

Hand to the Plough

A Personal Record

H. CECIL PAWSON

M.B.E., D.SC., F.R.S.E.,

Emeritus Professor of Agriculture of the Universities of Durham and Newcastle

DENHOLM HOUSE PRESS

NUTFIELD · REDHILL · SURREY · RH1 4HW

First published 1973

© Denholm House Press 1973

ISBN 0 85213 066 x

Printed by Cox & Wyman Ltd
London, Reading and Fakenham

CONTENTS

ACKNOWLEDGEMENTS

I am deeply thankful to my wife for all her encouragement, her wise counsel, and for the fact that, until acute illness finally prevented it, she did most of the typing of the MS. My warm thanks are due to Miss Pamela Smith, a friend of many years, who then gave invaluable help in continuing the typescript, and also to Mr. Wm. Hoggard, Secretary of Newcastle Y.M.C.A., who arranged for Miss Rita Martin to re-type four chapters. To Mr. Aubrey Smith, the Publishers' Editor; and to his colleague Rev. Paul Morton-George, M.A., who undertook the major task of reducing the original manuscript to the form in which it appears; to my son, the Rev. J. D. Pawson, M.A., B.Sc., who helped in the choice of the title; and to other friends, going back to the time years ago when my great friend the Rev. Dr. Leslie Church (one time Editor of the Epworth Press) requested this book, I am abidingly grateful; also to the Editor of the *Methodist Recorder*, and to Mr. Maxwell Deas, Director of Religious Programmes, Tyne-Tees Television Ltd.

There are so many friends who have contributed in one way or another to the experiences expressed in this book that it would be impossible to list them, but for them all I am truly grateful.

H. CECIL PAWSON

PUBLISHERS' NOTE

This book by Professor H. Cecil Pawson, M.B.E.,
D.Sc., F.R.S.E., Emeritus Professor of Agriculture
of the Universities of Durham and Newcastle, is a personal
account by a man distinguished both in his chosen
career and also in religious life. We are sorry that we
found it necessary, in fulfilling the main purpose of
the book, to omit many personal items which appeared in
the original manuscript.

These include references to Dr. Pawson's many friends,
his broadcasting and writing, and his leisure pursuits.

Prologue

Nervously I knocked on the door of the Headmaster's private room. A penetrating voice said: 'Come in.' The Head was seated at his desk and I stood before him in wondering awe. A pause, which seemed endless, and then the voice I had perforce always accepted as authoritative: 'Well, Pawson, this is your last day at the school.' 'Yes, Sir,' I replied, not sure whether it was meant to be a question or a statement of fact. Another pause, then, with eyes which seemed as penetrating as his voice, he said: 'Well, Pawson, you're not brilliant but you're a slogger, and if you'll keep it up, you'll get there. Good morning,' and I withdrew. It was as short as that!

Forty-five years later, when I retired, I recalled these last words of my Headmaster and asked myself: 'I wonder what he had in mind when he said: "You'll get there"?' Was he thinking simply of material wealth, social position, political or industrial fame? Or had he in mind something deeper and finer than what mere money can buy or power over others secure? Later on, when I sat where he sat, metaphorically speaking, I was informed more than once by parents discussing the progress of my past students: 'Oh, yes, he's made good. He has a fine position now, earning £4,000 a year and further prospects.' What does it really mean 'to make good'? or 'to get there'? This book is a personal record of an increasing discovery of what I believe was God's answer for me.

1

Heritage

'Yea, I have a goodly heritage' (*Psalm 16: 6*).
*'It was the Christ incarnate in my mother that made
me desire to be a Christian. It was the passion of my
father's prayers that made me long to preach'* –
A. T. Guttery.

'What part of Yorkshire, sir?'

The questioner was one of my audience at a meeting up the Tyne Valley. He went on to explain that he made a hobby of detecting the county or area from which a speaker originated by his accent or dialect. He said he had not found it easy in my case, but two or three times when I got excited, he thought he located me.

'Where do *you* think?' I said.

'I should say somewhere in the West Riding, say Leeds area.'

'Well, I've never lived in Yorkshire, but my father was born in Wakefield and lived there until in his twenties. My mother was born on a farm eight miles north of Doncaster and lived there until she married at thirty years of age, so you're not far out, are you?'

I had spent only a few holidays at Wakefield as a boy with my grandparents. In later years I came to love Northumberland – a county much underestimated by most southerners – it is of rich interest historically, scenically and agriculturally. More than sixty years of my life have been spent on Tyneside. Yet, whenever I travel into Yorkshire, I have a strange feeling compounded of special interest and

9

pleasure. It is not just that I love its beautiful dales, its glorious moors and coastline, nor that I was interested from early days in discussion of its outstanding cricket prowess and later discovered its variety of farming interest. No doubt all these contribute to this feeling, but there is something more. Its essence must surely be the ingrained knowledge that this is where my forbears lived and served and died, bequeathing an inheritance of things more valuable and important by far than money, which heritage has enriched my life all my days.

I had long held John Pawson in high esteem as one of John Wesley's inner circle of preachers and friends. A visit to Somerset House moved me to write to the Vicar of the Parish Church at Thorner, who made an extensive search, which resulted in a full list of Pawsons. My friend Rev. Dr. Maldwyn Edwards, whom I have long regarded as the authority on the Wesleys and early Methodists, wrote as follows:

'I have no doubt at all that it is from this line, the nephew of John Pawson, that you must trace your ancestry. I am convinced that since the name of Pawson is so rare (I know of no other case in our ministry) and since your father, D. Ledger Pawson, knew himself to be a Methodist of many generations, you are descended from this particular line.'

I visited his grave in the churchyard at Thorner (a few miles to the west of the A1), and copied these words from the tombstone: 'John Pawson who died 19th March 1806, aged 68, 44 years an eminent minister among the people called Methodists and his hallowed name without the poet's praise or sculptor's toil shall live in future days.

'Art thou a stranger to a name so dear?
Think not to find its sacred history here.
Go ask the Church to which his life was given.
Nor ask alone but follow him to heaven.'

John Pawson wrote of John Wesley: 'He acted the part of a father to me on all occasions, so that I shall for ever have cause to praise the Lord on his account.'

My Pawson grandparents, when I first remember them, had retired from business and lived at Wakefield. My grandfather is described as a 'Worsted Spinner (Journeyman)' on my father's birth certificate. They lived very simply, though having plenty of dry bread and black treacle, with butter only on Sundays. It was a poor home in material things, yet so hospitable, as befitted the fine Christians my grandparents were, that it was nicknamed 'The Methodist Inn'. My grandfather would earn a weekly wage of about a pound. When he brought home his weekly wage, my grandmother would put into one basin the rent, etc., in a second basin so much for their church needs, and in a third what remained for food and clothing. She brought up a family of three sons, two of whom became Methodist ministers, and the third a devoted Methodist choirmaster.

After some years of married life, my grandfather, fulfilling a desire of many years, decided to become his own master. One day he arrived home in great excitement, to inform my grandmother in a torrent of eloquence that he had found what he wanted. It was a corner house in a row which possessed a shop window, a spacious backyard etc., situated in a village near the town of Wakefield, which is called Thornes. When at last she managed to get a word in, she asked one question. Not 'Henry, is it in a good neighbourhood for the children?' or 'Are there good prospects for developing the business' and so on. No, her first question was: 'Henry, how far is it from the chapel?' She was thinking first and foremost of how far the family would have to walk for Sunday worship and, in particular, the distance her three boys would have to walk to Sunday School as well as to other services.

My grandmother Pawson lived until she was 75, always

helping others to the end of her days. On the gravestone in West Parade Methodist burial ground adjoining the church, these words are inscribed: 'She hath done what she could'. Though spare in frame and never robust, and subject in later years to recurrent heart attacks, she fully justified the description written on the tombstone of an American woman, who constantly served others beyond what her friends thought physically possible, namely: 'She hath done what she *couldn't*.'

A few years later, in 1913, my grandfather, aged 79 years, followed her. Sixteen years later my father, in his last illness wrote out clear instructions that under his name on the gravestone the following words should be inscribed:– 'What a Meeting!' As John Wesley said of the Methodists of his day: 'Our people die well'.

For my mother, the story began in 1863, its setting a simple, homely looking farmhouse in a tiny hamlet and just across a narrow lane from the little church and God's acre. Here on Christmas Day, she was born. Grandfather Kitchen was a good farmer, able to make and save some money because of his great industry and thrift, but like more than one business man I have met, whilst expert in his own line, he was extremely credulous when investing his savings. He once purchased some houses shown to him by a clever rogue who, it was subsequently discovered, had never owned the properties. A Methodist local preacher, he often, because of his work-filled days, had to fall back on an old, favourite sermon, and this, so I was told, was an exposition of 'Go to the ant, thou sluggard; consider her ways and be wise . . .' (Proverbs 6: 6). He was no 'gentleman farmer' but worked as hard, if not harder, than any of his helpers.

Grandmother Kitchen I never knew in any direct way but the picture I formed was of a gracious, kindly, devoted Christian. Above everything, she was sacrificially generous.

For church causes, for instance Missionary work, she would save by giving up sugar in her tea and in other ways, but outstanding, as my mother often recounted, were her personal gifts to the poor and needy. Not only was she of the kind who 'let not their right hand know what their left hand doeth', but she often concealed from my grandfather gifts of food and money she made to those who came to the farmhouse kitchen door. From time to time he found out and would then proceed to inform her in no uncertain way that she would ruin him and the family, but apparently it had little effect and she would soon return to her generous ways.

Soon after my mother was born, my grandfather took over another farm adjoining the one already described; this was situated on the main road (now known as the A1) and called Robin Hood's Well. I shall never forget the shock I experienced when, in quite recent years, I came to the spot where I always looked eagerly for sight of my mother's girlhood home to find that both house and farm buildings had completely vanished. Everything had been bulldozed to make possible the wide, new double-track, which a few miles south becomes the Doncaster By-pass. The old well from which the farm got its name has been re-erected, but no trace of the farmhouse remains.

Every Sunday morning my grandparents would walk along a footpath through the fields to the little Church of England to attend and participate in the service of Holy Communion. In the evening the living-room in their own home – namely the large kitchen – was the meeting place and preaching place of the Methodist Society of which they were ardent, faithful members unto their journey's end. No one will ever make me believe this kitchen was not fully consecrated to the glory of God, though no bishop had pronounced it so.

For very many years, when motoring to London, either going or on the return journey, I would turn off the main road at the sign marked Skelbrook (the name later chosen by my father and mother for the house to which they retired) and in a mile and a half arrive at the hamlet with the little church where in the churchyard these two faithful servants of God were laid to rest. Seldom do I meet anyone as I make my way into the little church which remains the same, for a quiet prayer of thanksgiving for my inheritance. Then coming out, in a few yards I am standing at the grave. Here on the stone are the usual particulars, namely of birth and death, and then words which never fail to convey their message to me of peace and fulfilment:

'So He bringeth them to their desired haven.'

Beyond question is that my paternal and maternal grandparents were Yorkshire folk of staunch, loyal, Methodist Christian convictions. My grandparents on both sides made possible for me what is truly 'a goodly heritage'.

What I owe to my parents is incalculable and to remember them and the privileges of the Christian home in which I was brought up is ever to be challenged by the Master's words: 'Unto whomsoever much is given, of him shall be much required . . .' No home could have given more of the wealth that abides of truth, beauty and goodness than mine afforded to me and continually, through the years, I have thanked God for every remembrance of my parents.

What an amazing record of service for the Church and the Kingdom of God lies behind my father's thirty-seven years' work as a minister! It was service expressed in utter giving of himself in love to God and in love to His children. Though he was translated to the higher service in 1934, hardly ever a fortnight passes to date without someone expressing to me a grateful memory of his life and ministry. As one man said recently: 'Your father didn't so much preach people into the Kingdom as love them into it.'

The morning after the all-important event of his decision for Christ, he was behind the counter packing up groceries for a customer when he was suddenly assailed by a tremendous temptation – and this is how the tempter proceeded: 'You are not saved, you only went forward to the communion rail because some of your friends did. You were carried away by your emotions. You were swept off your feet by the eloquence of the preacher. It doesn't mean a thing, you are no different this morning to what you were on Saturday'. All this raged (I feel this is the right word) through my father's mind and heart as he tied up the parcel and counted out the change. When the customer had gone, my father opened the door leading from the shop to the living-room and stood beside a clock affixed to the wall. 'Well, Devil, you say I did not come to Christ last night? His promise is that "him that cometh unto me, I will in no wise cast out", and I am coming now, this morning (and glancing at the clock) at exactly eleven o'clock, and you cannot stop me.' It was then he received the blessed gift of assurance, 'The Spirit himself beareth witness with our spirit that we are the children of God' (Romans 8: 16.). My father told me that he had had many temptations down the years, but that Monday morning one never returned. To the last moments of his earthly life he was sure of that which matters most and which was the secret of his glorious life, namely: 'Blessed assurance, Jesus is mine.'

For many years I have had the habit once a year of going off for a whole day on my own. I decided to spend one such day at my father's home town of Wakefield. Arriving there, I felt a keen desire to find the shop and house at Thornes which I had never seen. I stood stock still and wondered which way to take, having no address about which I could inquire. There was no magic voice, but I *knew* I should turn left and soon after passing under a railway arch, I saw at the end of one of the streets a corner shop. I looked into the window, not very prepossessing, and then walked in and spoke to the woman behind the counter.

'I wonder if you would mind telling me how long you have lived here'. She told me.

'And who did you take over from when you came?' She told me, and I repeated the same question more than once, slightly modified:

'And who did they succeed?'

I felt a keen disappointment in her replies, then, almost without hope, I said for the last time:

'I don't suppose you can go any further back, can you?'

'Well,' she said, 'it's a very long time ago, but I can just remember one other, I think they were called Pawson, and all I remember hearing about them is that they had three or four sons and I believe two of them became parsons'.

'Thank you so very much. One last question, if I am not troubling you too much.' Pointing to a door, I said: 'Does that lead to a back room?'

'Yes,' she replied, and opening it, showed me her living-room. A little dazed with sheer excitement, I said:

'There's not a clock on the wall, is there?'

'No, but there's one on the mantelpiece.' The clock had gone, but the room was the same, the room where my father had won his spiritual battle.

The end of my father's earthly life revealed the grandeur of his faith in God and the glory of his Christian convictions. After a period of disquieting physical weakness, he was given an X-ray examination and taken to a nursing home pending an operation. After the operation he never recovered consciousness but lay for some days before his soul departed this life.

He left a writing pad which I was to read if he did not recover, I treasure it beyond words. In it he had written each day a letter addressed to 'The Lord Jesus Christ'. The last one, 'Sunday morning, January 15th, 1934', is shorter than the others and finishes with these words:

'I am not complaining if this be deemed suffering, because Thou art making good the promise so richly, that the grace balances the need. Blessed Lord, Thou wilt be with me all through the day, as I pass through this new experience. I have not passed this way before.

Must close now – nurse is waiting.

"Thou wilt keep him in perfect peace whose mind is stayed on Thee."

Yours lovingly,

D. Ledger Pawson.'

From time to time I am asked to write in an autograph book, and often the request includes the words, 'Your father wrote in it'. My reply is always the same.

'I'll tell you before I open the book what he wrote. He either wrote: "He whose sermon is a godly life will never preach too long" or "If the outlook is bad, try the uplook" '.

He never really retired, but continued after becoming supernumerary to take Sunday and weeknight services in various churches, visiting the sick in hospital and home, meeting and helping discharged prisoners, visiting magistrates courts to be of help to any in need. In short, he continued the work of evangelism which he had done so effectively for over half a century. He continued to play

and enjoy his weekly game of golf and to go to St. James'
Park to see Newcastle United play football.

I never knew his equal in talking about supernatural
things in such a natural way and in speaking of his Master
here, there and everywhere, as the Spirit gave him utterance.
Of the scores of incidents I could recount, here is a typical
one. He went to have a word with one of his Mission
members who was head of one of the departments in Bain-
bridges's stores. Spotting my father, the gentleman concerned excused himself from a young couple who were
inspecting carpets, to come and speak to him, and whispered
that his possible customers were engaged and were choosing
carpets for their intended home. My father waved him aside
and said: 'I can wait for you'. Later the salesman had to
leave the couple again to deal with a telephone call and
when he returned, found all three behind up-ended rolls of
carpet with head bowed as my father prayed for their future
happiness.

My mother takes the second place for the sole reason that
I know she would have it so. No one more clearly exempli-
fied the truth of our Lord's words: 'He that loseth his life for
my sake shall find it', than she did for Christ's sake in our
home. She lived to serve God by serving His children, beginning with her husband and children and then as many as she
could possibly help. J. M. Barrie, in his characteristically
whimsical style, once wrote: 'The God to whom a little boy
says his prayers has a face very like his mother's'. I know that
to be true.

I recall one unforgettable night, when she told me that
story of the green hill outside the city wall and what happened there so long ago. I was just a small boy and I don't
think I could have spelt the word 'atonement', much less say
what it meant, but I really came to know for the first time
that 'He loved me and gave Himself for me'. I always think

of that moment as my first response to Christ's wonderful love. Throughout a lifetime I have read scores of books on the life and death of Christ. Yet the love of Christ, as revealed through my mother's lips and life, has influenced all my increasing knowledge of the grandeur and glory of the greatest thing in God and the universe, namely the love of God revealed for all men and all time in 'Jesus Christ, the same yesterday, today and for ever'.

One of my friends, a Jewish Rabbi, once said that, important as was the Synagogue in the Jewish faith, the home was regarded as even more important. From my own experience there has come the abiding conviction that children are much more likely to find a home in the Church if they discover the Church in the home. It was so with me.

Infinitely precious to me is the very old Waterman pen used by my mother for many years. It is a constant reminder of how you can dedicate a pen to the glory of God. Although no public speaker, my mother could and did write innumerable, wonderful letters of comfort, guidance and blessing. Only God knows the number of people she blessed in this way. One example stands out vividly in my memory. At Christmas time every member of the family was commandeered for weeks in wrapping up parcels to send to friends she had made over the years in the various circuits where my father had ministered. What a welcome she would receive in heaven from so many friends she made and never forgot.

As I have always had a keen interest in beginnings, I never forgot the story of how she met my father for the first time. A number of young people had come over from Wakefield to a meeting in her home addressed by a missionary who, it would appear, gave such a rousing and inspiring address that it prompted a young man from Wakefield in the audience to express audible approval several times with such words as

'Praise the Lord', 'Amen' and 'Hallelujah'. After the meeting, my mother said to her sister: 'Who was the young man who rudely interrupted the speaker?' He subsequently became my father!

In latter years, my mother was handicapped by deafness, but she continued faithful in her service for God in comforting and blessing in so many ways anyone in need. Came the day when our family doctor advised taking another opinion. When the specialist was introduced, my mother said:

'Doctor, I believe in medical science and in prayer.'

'Good for you', said the consultant.

She became ill enough to be removed to a nursing home and after some time there I had an intuition that the time was not far distant when she would depart this life. I was sitting by her bedside one evening in the nursing home when I noticed a tear on my mother's face.

'Mother,' I said, 'would you like to go home?' – meaning her earthly home, which she loved so much. I knew then for certain that I had interpreted aright the tear. I doubt if she would have said what she did, if I had not been guided to put the question, but love is not blind, its sight is so often insight. The doctor demurred slightly, but I think in his heart he agreed, and an ambulance brought her to the bedroom she loved so well in the house next door to my own home. To see her face after she had been made comfortable in her own bed was a benediction of thanksgiving, which I shall never forget. A devoted friend, a fully trained nurse, ministered to her for the few remaining days of her earthly journey, but in those days she was peaceful and happy.

I can never repay the debt I owe to such parents and continually thank God that I was brought up in such a truly Christian home. How fully I agree with what Thomas Champress said. 'If our mothers sent in a bill for all we owe them then we should all be bankrupt.' The legacy of the

Christian Sunday, the daily reading of God's Word and prayers at the family altar my wife and I have sought to pass on to our own children, for no material blessings can ever compare with the spiritual wealth of such an inheritance.

2

Growing Up

'O happy home, where Thou art loved the dearest'.

A very old lady who well remembered my father, her one-time minister, told me that as deputy leader of my father's Society Class (as they were commonly described in the Methodist Church) she received a note on one occasion from him saying that he might be delayed in getting to the meeting, and asking if she would kindly take his place until he arrived. Later that evening a second note informed her that a baby boy had arrived at the Manse 'sound in wind and limb'. This was the first announcement of my coming into this world. It was in 1897, in Bristol.

What an immeasurable blessing to be born in a Christian home! I was one of four children, my sister Dorothy, the eldest, myself next and my two brothers, Edward and Arthur. No family, I dare to affirm, were and are more closely knit together. Edward was a dedicated Methodist organist, playing every Sunday at the church at Rowlands Gill where my sister Dolly (as we have always called her) is still a devoted member and worker at 78 years of age. Arthur, though greatly handicapped physically, became a Methodist Local Preacher before his untimely death at 40 years of age. I can confidently affirm that (although my dear wife, my two brothers and brother-in-law have joined my parents in heaven), to quote Charles Wesley, 'One family we dwell in Him'.

I have often asked of others: 'What is your earliest recollection?' I have no difficulty in recalling mine. I was sitting in my bedroom in our home in Newcastle in Rye Hill being nursed by our 'mother's help' (as they were then called), Miss Jay, and she was singing to me:

> 'A little ship was on the sea,
> It was a pretty sight.
> It sailed along so pleasantly,
> And all was calm and bright'.

Later, before being tucked into bed, I was taken to the window to listen to the sound of many voices coming from the great mission hall next door, where my father was minister, at a Sunday evening service, and I would be about two years old.

I can also dimly remember crowds of people shouting, cheering, waving flags and processing along Newcastle's Scotswood Road at the bottom of Rye Hill. I was told it was 'Mafeking'. I must then have been three years old. At a later date, when still too young to attend an evening service, we 'played at services' and, as the eldest son, I was often the preacher. A large easy chair, reversed, made a convenient pulpit. In it I kept a few cushions and if any member of the congregation showed signs of lack of interest or sleepiness, I used to 'let them have one', an action which never failed to arouse or arrest attention!

In very few years the pattern of my Sunday was determined, namely: morning service, afternoon Sunday School, evening service followed by the prayer meeting. No doubt it is true that 'distance lends enchantment to the view', but I cannot recall feeling that Sunday was a dull or boring day. There were also interesting books to be read, some largely pictorial, which kindled imagination, and hymn singing which has remained a lasting joy.

Parsons' sons are not born saints – as some in my boyhood

days were half inclined to think. Sooner or later they realize they need to be saved as much as anyone else from the things which outrage conscience. Some time in the first eight years of my life I told my first lie – an experience I never forgot. It happened on a Sunday, and the means of temptation my usual Saturday income – a penny – and a Jewish shop not far away in Rye Hill. The sweets you could obtain for a farthing or two were remarkable. I never dreamed of spending my penny all at once!

That fateful Sunday, I not only changed my penny but purchased some sweets. The cynic may smile, the psychologist enlarge on the guilt complex and the like, but the fact remains that I acted a lie and deceived my parents. For the rest of the day, I was utterly miserable and kept out of my father's sight. But I could not got to bed without confessing with shame that I had deceived him. Never shall I forget the look on his face! How I wished he had give me a hard whipping, but he never laid a hand on me. His sad face just bore the look of disappointed, wronged love and *I knew it*. I remember he said: 'I forgive you, but you need God's forgiveness, so let us pray and ask Him to forgive you and help you always to be truthful'. Then and there we knelt together and though I have never forgotten the sin, I can remember also to this day the wonderful feeling of having things put right with God and my father. I had never heard of the word absolution, and if I had, I wouldn't have understood it, but that Sunday evening, so long ago, I experienced it.

When old enough to remain with my mother to the prayer meeting at the conclusion of the Sunday evening service, I used to watch men and women from different parts of the hall make their way down the aisles past the rostrum and go through a green baize door to what was called 'the inquiry room' in response to my father's invitation. I recall asking my mother where they were going, and her reply: 'They are going to meet with Jesus'. Being just a child, I really thought Jesus, in bodily form, must be beyond that door. Now that I am a man, like Paul, I have put away many childish things but not that one, save to hold it with a larger and truer concept of its reality. All through my life I have seen men and women – young and old – meet with Jesus and prove the truth of His own words: 'Blessed are they that have not seen and yet have believed.'

Here, then, was the environment in which I spent the first eight years of my life. This was the lowest part of Newcastle in every sense, with the great Armstrong (now Vickers) works on one side of Scotswood Road, and on the other side mostly mean shops and a record number of public houses for any city. From Scotswood Road, stretching up the steep hill were numerous streets of houses of the same monotonous pattern. No wonder so many found that the quickest way of escape from slumdom was to get drunk! All this area has been cleared in recent years and skyscraper flats with trees and green borders have replaced the slums I knew not only as a boy but for many years thereafter.

Simple, inexpensive games and toys were the rule in those days, but I well remember my first rocking-horse which, though so much cheaper in those days than now, was thought of as a great luxury. Christmas and birthdays were, as they still are, the great days for presents. Pillow-cases rather than stockings were hung on one's bed at Christmas, and although we did not know poverty, not much money came into a Methodist Manse, yet the pillowcases were always full. We were allowed 'one dip' before the morning Christmas Church Service; then after the Christmas dinner we all sat in a family circle and each took turns in un-wrapping a gift. This tradition has been followed in my own family.

Muffin-men, German bands, the barrel organ with the

monkey holding the collecting box were familiar sights of those days, as also fine dogs on main railway station platforms collecting for charities. Pierrots and Punch and Judy shows on the sands were more common than today, with donkeys, occasionally replaced with ponies.

Those were the days of the much dreaded Workhouse. A lady helper at the Mission used to visit the old women every week and one day asked what they would like her to read. "Give us something with a bit of love in it, Miss," was the reply. A happy contrast is afforded today by Eventide Homes and as a Methodist I take especial pride in the Methodist Homes for the Aged and those of the Methodist Local Preachers Mutal Aid Association.

Staying with our Wakefield grandparents in those far off days, I remember how we would rush into the house in Ings Road and then cautiously look out through the front window as a procession of men, handcuffed and chained, were escorted from the railway station along the road to the prison – no conveyance by prison vans in those days.

It was a tough world in many ways but I early became conscious of the good folk who sought to bring blessings to those in need. The Mission environment was made up of activities to brighten the lives of the aged and infirm and the poor, the cripples and others who had failed in the battle of life. It is sheer nonsense to imagine that men like my father preached only 'pie in the sky'. He led a band of men and women mission workers who sought to demonstrate by loving, sharing and sacrificial service the whole Gospel for the whole man, and to do whatever they could to tackle the problem of social inequalities and injustices.

Lantern lectures were our chief public entertainments. The moving picture, or film, did not come into my recreations until I was a schoolboy at Whitley Bay and I went to see the first 'pictures' (as they were described) in the old

Baths, which had been boarded over to take the seats for the audience. Piano accompaniment was the only addition to the silent film which in the exciting parts, when the distressed heroine was delivered from her kidnappers by the hero who galloped away bearing the rescued maiden, used to rise to a crescendo (always the same tune) to fit in with the galloping horses pursued by the kidnappers.

At the foot of Rye Hill was a pillar-box to which I was frequently sent to post letters. If it was dark, I used to run back in the middle of the road after slipping in the letters, not only because I possessed a nervous temperament, but on account of brutal and beastly scenes I witnessed outside the public house at the bottom of the road. Such scenes which I dreaded I am sure my friend the Rev. Dr. Leslie Weatherhead believes account in some measure, as a kind of psychological throwback, for my life-long abstinence from alcohol and advocacy of temperance.

One example was given to me by the late Lord Rank – another life-long abstainer. Many years ago, he suffered a very serious illness in which Lord Dawson (then physician to H.M. King George V) was called in as consultant. He found Lord Rank in a very critical condition. Happily the patient responded to the treatment he prescribed, namely a teaspoonful of brandy every few hours. Later when Lord Rank was convalescent, Lord Dawson congratulated him on his recovery and said: 'I could not have saved your life if you had not been a total abstainer from alcohol.'

I was greatly influenced, in those early years of my life, by men and women who were converted in the Mission, and can recall many such characters to this day. The first of these was Geordie, a boiler-maker, earning £10 a week, a high wage in those days, at Armstrong Works, but spending nearly all his money on vices. Gambling was one of his great passion, and on greyhounds and racing pigeons, race-horses, and a young man whom he trained for flat racing, he gambled heavily. A man told me he remembered Geordie persuading a fellow-workman to gamble with him on two flies crawling up a wall as to which would reach the top first.

'He would gamble on anything,' he said.

This was but one of the habits which enslaved him and reduced his home to poverty.

Somehow my father managed to persuade him to attend a Men's Meeting at the People's Hall, and seven weeks later the miracle happened – Geordie was converted. This wonderful experience of Christ in his life not only resulted in completely changed conduct, but his face actually became transformed, and Geordie the tough, hardened, swearing, drinking Tynesider became one of God's gentlemen, tender-hearted and loving, as I can testify. When Geordie began his Christian life, he could neither read nor write. My father taught him, amongst other things, to say the Lord's Prayer.

Some time after his conversion, Geordie discovered that the young man he had once maintained for flat racing was dying of tuberculosis. He went immediately to see him and found him lying in a dirty, fireless attic. He went out, and in a few minutes returned with coal and other parcels. After lighting a fire and making things more comfortable, Geordie sat down to talk and as he did so, he became convinced that he ought to speak to the sick man about his soul, but somehow he couldn't begin. At last he rose to go.

'Ah, well, Aa'll away! Aa'll be back the morn. S'long.'

Then the young man said: 'Thanks for all the things ye've fetched us. Mind you, it was a grand thing for ye when 'ee got converted, Geordie.'

'By, it was an' aal,' replied Geordie. 'The Lord's made a mighty change i' my life.'

'He has that. Aa wish He'd dee the same fer me!'

'Wey, ax Him, man, an' He will. Shall aa gan an' fetch somebody to taak to ye that knaas mair nor me?'

'Nam na, Geordie, hinney, aa want nebody but ye.'

'Wey, ax Him yersel', then.'

'Ay, but aa diven't knaa how to pray.'

'Well, just say the Lord's Prayer after me.' Geordie knelt beside the sick man and together they prayed the Lord's Prayer several times.

Two days later, though the patient was clearly much weaker, Geordie was met by a smiling face and the glad news: 'He's done for me, Geordie, what He did for thee.' It had happened whilst all alone he had been praying the Lord's Prayer.

My second character was a cabman, always called by his friends Tot. He had the reputation of being one of the hardest drinking men on Newcastle Central Station Cab Stand. He drank so heavily one night that the publican, wanting to be rid of him, promised two men free beer if they would land Tot home in the nearby street. When Tot awoke out of his drunken stupor, he found he had been robbed of several pounds and – to a cabman – his indispensable watch, for in those days public clocks were not so numerous as today. He realized what a fool he was and resolved to rid himself of this sinful habit. He found his way to the People's Hall, Rye Hill, and there found the new life which Christ offers to every man. My father once told me that for thirty years thereafter, Tot lived such a consistent, faithful, Christian life that he never gave his minister five minutes anxiety about his progress.

Soon after his conversion, Tot was seen running after a gentleman. When he arrived back at the stand, a fellow cabman said:

'Was he trying to *do* ye, Tot?'

'No, he gave me half a soverign over and above the fare.'

'You don't mean to say you took the half quid back, do you?'

'Yes,' said Tot. 'I thought he only meant to give me sixpence for a tip.' Nothing more was said then, but next day when some of the cabmen were chaffing Tot about becoming a Christian, the inquirer of the day before stepped forward.

'Shut up, you chaps. The next man that says owt more against Tot and his religion, I'll fell him. If religion will make Tot Reed give up half a quid for sixpence, there's something in it.'

After his conversion, Tot longed for his wife to share his wonderful experience of Christ's love. She had shared with him in many a drunken orgy. It was not to be, for though he sought for this crowning blessing for his home earnestly and long, he could not persuade her to become a Christian. Indeed he had to endure such taunts and conduct with obscene language from her, and some of her associates, because of his Christian life, that my father said his home was often like hell. It was Jesus who said 'a man will find his enemies under his own roof', as the New English Bible translates it. Three times he went to sign the papers making possible a separation, but each time he laid aside the pen, and said:

'I cannot do it. I encouraged her in my sinful days, and with all her persecution, I love her still.'

Many other memories crowd my mind concerning those days in a City Manse. The sight of a crowded lower hall (of the People's Hall) for a Christmas party for crippled children. The sight of the ugly, weighty irons which had to be worn by some of them, the crutches and rather crude wheeled chairs sent me home moved with heartfelt pity, yet also impressed with their cheerfulness and obvious enjoyment of the party. Saturday mornings, standing by my father as from a large tub he baled out hot soup and from a clothes basket distributed chunks of bread to poor people, who brought their cups and bowls; in those days there was plenty of unemployment and consequent poverty and no public assistance or old age pensions. Young as I was, I felt sure that much, if not all, of the soup would go to the little children clinging to their mothers' skirts. I have lived long enough to recognize how limited is the power of legislation to change the inborn, selfish, sinful nature of man, but I am also conscious and profoundly grateful for the Welfare State and for the fact that today there are no starving people and boys and girls were never better nourished than now.

Just before the outbreak of the Second World War, I was tutor to two married, well-educated Indians, who were studying for a higher degree at what is now the University of Newcastle. In a conversation I had with them, not long before they returned to India, I asked what was their main impression of this country having lived here for two years. After a pause, Singh replied: 'I think I shall tell my people that the main difference between England and India is that you have no hungry people', and Chaudri concurred.

This was at a time when we had between 2 and 3 million people 'on the dole', so I expressed my doubt, saying that not far from where I lived in Newcastle there were people who would go to the butcher's shop with literally a shilling or two and ask him to do his best for that sum. Then one of my Indian friends replied: 'But, sir, you don't understand – we mean starving people. For example, it is a common sight with us as we walk along a road, to see a figure ahead of us stumble and fall, and when we come to the spot to find a few rags covering a body in which the ribs are all sticking out of the flesh of one who has just died. We have never seen that sight in England.' I was always grateful thereafter that when

I read of vast shortages of rice in India, this conversation enabled me to see human faces in statistics and helped me to pray and serve more effectively the hungry and homeless in the poorer countries.

But it was not all grime, poverty, slums and, for my parents, days of arduous self-giving in the service of so many of the most needy of God's children. Every Monday morning, my father had his game of golf on the free course (as it was then) on the Town Moor, Newcastle, and to the end of his days he enjoyed if not a weekly game, as often as opportunity allowed.

For the family, there was the occasional visit – usually for half a day – to the seaside by train from Newcastle to Tynemouth to Whitley Bay and from time to time the hire of the milkman's horse, the milk cart being replaced by a far from new governess trap, as it was described, to take us all eight to ten miles into the country. I remember on one occasion, after about two miles, we encountered a steam traction engine and a gang of men engaged on road repairs. This was too much for our horse which reared and bucked and refused to pass the ugly monster. My mother was so frightened (even though a farmer's daughter), or should I say concerned about her crying young family, that she prevailed on Father to take us all home.

The most blessed memories are all associated with our family annual summer holiday and centred in one place. Salters Gate, with its house surrounded by heather moors, in contrast to Rye Hill, was indeed heaven to our young hearts and eyes, but let me try to explain what was sheer ecstasy.

It began with the stopping of a train on a single track line by a solitary signal, and stepping out on to a high chair provided by the signalman's wife as a substitute platform.

As soon as the train had left, we gazed upon what seemed

to us an interminable vista of heather moor, plantations and hill farms. The air in contrast to that of smoky Tyneside seemed unbelievably fresh. A mere hundred yards or so away was a single row of stone-built cottages, surrounded by the more close grazed green sward which soon gave place to the dominant heather, with the exception of one or two small fields to the west which provided hay and grazing and included a cow byre for the game-keeper's cow and calves. The lower two cottages had been turned into one dwelling place, called a shooting box. Next door was the game-keeper's house. In one of the remaining cottages one could buy from an old lady with an extremely limited selection, some bottled sweets and bars of chocolate. The top house (for the row was built on a gentle slope) had been transformed into a Methodist Chapel.

I must now explain how it was we came year after year to spend a fortnight at the double cottage at the end of the row.

Salters Gate was the shooting lodge owned by Mr. T. H. Bainbridge who with his brother owned one of the first ever Department Stores. He was joint Treasurer of my father's Mission. He loaned it to us for a fortnight. The isolation of our holiday home spelt for us children freedom and change (two essentials of a good holiday). We no longer turned on a tap for water but daily took turns to go along a track in the heather to fill cans – and usually our mouths first – with sparkling, clear, fresh water ceaselessly gushing forth from a spring. Wood logs provided the fuel; bilberries from a sparse, open plantation made lovely pies. Milk and butter from the game-keeper's cows, rabbits or an occasional game bird with some garden potatoes and vegetables – all tasted different from those bought in a shop. We also enjoyed, as my photograph album reminds me, helping with the haymaking – no scones, country butter and mugs of tea were so enjoyed as in the hayfield. It has to be admitted, however, that my youngest brother, when taken to the byre to watch the gamekeeper's wife do the milking (the first time he had ever seen a cow milked) refused his glass of milk at supper, saying he couldn't drink it if it came from the cow, but only from the shop or dairy, and drink it he would not until we returned to the city!

A source of endless pleasure was a shooting pony thoughtfully provided by Mr. Bainbridge. As the butcher called but once a week, and the bread and other stores the same, and the delivery of letters was only a few times a week, the pony was seldom inactive save on Sundays. We used to ride for a few miles over the moor to Waskerley for the nearest Post Office and, for general shopping, harness him to a flat cart in which to drive, seated on an orange box, to the nearest market town of Tow Law (County Durham). No State carriage at the Royal Mews could have been more wonderful than our Salters Gate flat cart! What great days these were. The family was often augmented by one or two relations or friends.

One of these friends I recall on a return visit to Salters Gate nearly ten years later, by which time I had become a college student, was my lecturer in Agricultural Botany. I still think of his brief visit as an 'eye-opener'. He was a very able botanist, a somewhat reserved bachelor, to whom I took a particular liking because of his patience and understanding with me. I asked my mother on one vacation if I might invite him to spend a few days with us at Salters Gate. She readily agreed and, somewhat to my surprise, but greatly to my delight, he just as readily accepted.

I directed him to get out at the station at Waskerley, and I walked over the moors to meet him. We had hardly left the hamlet of Waskerley before we were on the moorland track. Slung round his shoulders was a tin box, and suddenly he dived into the rank growth around us and picked a flower.

'Do you know what that is, Pawson?'

I had to admit ignorance. Then followed the name, Latin and English, and a description of the plant, and then the specimen was transferred to the tin box. He must have stopped scores of times on the walk, and his excitement in search and discovery were contagious, though more than once I despaired of reaching the end of the journey! Later I remember reflecting that I had walked over the very same track to meet him and never saw, save in a general way, the various wild flowers and plants he introduced to me.

The Manse dog who went with us on holiday – a general favourite – was a fox terrier called Prince. He had a curious habit, when excited, of trying to catch his short stub of a tail. Round and round he would go, without success until occasionally he could come against a chair leg and, screwing himself up, grab hold, no doubt giving it a sharp bite. An episode in the life of Prince is another memory of a very lovable companion.

Whilst the family were on a brief holiday at Blackpool, we children, with Prince, were taken one evening to the magic Play Fair at the South Shore. Before the evening was over, we discovered to our heart-rending dismay that Prince was lost. Searching until dark, we became utterly weary, and finally returned to our lodgings to a night of tearful mourning for a lost companion. We returned after the holiday believing that we had seen the last of dear old Prince.

A year later, we were again in Blackpool. Though no dog had taken Prince's place, time had dulled our sense of loss. Again we found ourselves at the South Shore. We came to the Water Chute and stood watching a boat come down. When it was near the bottom, we suddenly saw a dog leap off the prow into the water, swim towards the ascending boat, not waiting for the down boat to reach the landing stage.

Great were the cheers for the dog, and then suddenly recognition – or was it hope? – filled our hearts. We waited breathlessly for the next boat to come down, and when the dog leaped, we all yelled:

'Prince!'

He turned his head, looked somewhat dazed, then swam directly to us, leapt on the parapet splashing us all with water, then began to go round and round after his tail, thereby affirming his identity. I think my father must have given a fair financial reward and we returned home with the long lost companion of the family circle.

The closing years of my father's ministry at the People's Hall were clouded over by a serious breakdown in his health. He had contracted tubercular laryngitis. The consultants said there was little hope, but his one chance was to go immediately to a sanatorium in Switzerland.

On arrival in London, he was cared for by my mother's sister, who lived there, and saw him into a compartment of the boat train at Victoria. Greatly distressed by his condition, and feeling that he was too ill to make the journey she scanned the platform for any intending passenger who might help in some way. She stopped a Salvation Army officer and told him that her brother-in-law, who had never been abroad in his life, was so very ill and would have to deal with luggage, customs, passport, etc.

'Take me to him, Madam,' he said.

He found a seat near him, and said to my aunt: 'Now don't worry about anything. I am going to the station where he makes his last change before Davos-Platz, where you say he will be met by the Sanatorium staff. I will see to everything until then.'

As the train started, my father got out his Bible (which I still treasure) and underlined a verse.

'May I see what you have marked?' said his kindly travelling companion, and my father showed him: 'And Jacob went on his way and the angels of God met him.'

My father made a wonderful recovery. He had the will to get well if it was God's will, and great faith in prayer and co-operation with his doctors. When he had left us, he weighed well under 10 stones, but on his return he arrived early and sat waiting on a seat on the railway platform. He had increased so much in weight and was so changed in appearance that without showing any sign of recognition, he allowed us children to walk past him, take a passing glance and fail to know him. How great was our rejoicing when he called to us and we recognized his voice!

The German doctor told my father that he was cured, but must never preach again. My father replied that that was like saying to a bird, 'You must never fly again.' On his return, he decided after a few months to begin again and try a country circuit where, of necessity, he would have to spend much time in the fresh air. Thus it came about that the family, now happily re-united, found themselves in a new home, this time in the Manse at Bakewell, Derbyshire.

Perhaps it ought rather to be described as a manse in a country market town, for that is a true description of Bakewell when the Pawson family took up residence there in 1909. To the younger members, however, after living on Tyneside, Bakewell was a complete and delightful contrast to the smoky factories and congested slum houses and streets we had left behind. Not far away was the stately mansion of Chatsworth House, whilst nearer still was the romantic Haddon Hall. All around was the lovely, peaceful countryside. The Manse itself was set in a most pleasant garden, overlooking a field, and possessing what to us boys presented exciting possibilities, namely a stable and coach-house. Here at Bakewell began my last and most important school period at the Lady Manners Grammar School, and I always believe that the years spent at this school contained the most lasting impressions and influences of my education.

One of the first developments we persistently urged upon my father when we got settled in the new manse was the making of a poultry house and run near the bottom of the garden. The next thing was to secure some poultry. Our friend, Mr. Tom Bainbridge, had a most beautiful country house and estate at Eshott, some twenty miles from Newcastle. Here he kept pedigree White Wyandottes – 'black and white', the colours of Newcastle United Football Club, as the boys of the Manse always thought of Eshott Home Farm. Half a dozen pullets duly arrived at Bakewell in the late summer as a present. I think we expected eggs the day after we put them into their new quarters. We had made a hole with a red hot poker in the door of the poultry house which gave us a view of the orange box which, with clean, attractive straw in its divisions, was provided to receive the eggs. We even, after some weeks, removed the white pot eggs from each nest and painted them brown, remembering that White Wyandottes always laid brown eggs. But all to no avail.

Then one day, when faith had gone and patience was almost exhausted, my mother made an announcement.

'When the pullets start to lay, we will have a rule to give all they lay on a Sunday to the sick and poor.'

Sure enough the first egg was laid the very next Sunday and my mother always maintained that they laid more on Sundays than on any other day, possibly because they were less disturbed by noise, the Manse being not far from the main road, and Sundays then were quiet days as compared with today.

The Manse poultry were destined to provide for myself and my brothers the first real problem in our prayer life. It happened as the result of our desire to have chickens as well as eggs, and we knew well enough that this meant buying a cock bird. We thereupon obtained a large, most handsome cockerel – White Wyandotte pedigree, of course – from the Salvation Farm Colony in Suffolk. Great indeed were our expectations from blending Salvation Army and Methodist blood! In due course, a pullet – now perhaps justifying the description of hen – went broody and was placed in a shady corner of the cellar of the Manse on a well prepared nesting box, holding a dozen eggs, and in confidence and hope we were already anticipating twelve lusty chicks.

The confidence was immeasurably fortified by reason of the fact that every night the three boys of the Manse, in their regular prayer, asked God to look after the hen and enable her to fulfil our highest expectations. It so happened that on our way to school we had to pass a butcher's shop, the owner of which often stood in the doorway, and being a friendly soul, would have a cheery word for us. One morning we confided to him our hopes and *prayers* concerning the 'sitting' hen. He was reputed, however, to be an atheist.

The great day arrived and on inspection one egg was found to have produced a live chick. Father thought that as the chickens were born, they should be removed from the hen. But mother (a farmer's daughter) maintained they should be left with her, and her counsel was adopted. The final result, after some days of dwindling hopes, was one live chicken and another crushed to death. The remaining eggs were addled. Our faith in prayer was greatly shaken and for several days we went the longer way round to school to miss seeing the butcher, but the time came when we knew that we must face him. Sure enough, he was there, and caught sight of us.

'Well, lads, how many chickens?'

'One' we replied and expected laughter and a sneer at our

prayers. To our astonishment he put his arms round my brother and myself.

'Never mind, lads, try again. You'll have better luck next time.'

In a strange, but not uncertain way, we believed God had influenced the butcher to treat us kindly in our keen disappointment.

Beyond all question, the most important experience of my days at Bakewell, and of my whole life, happened one week-night evening when I was thirteen years of age. I asked my father if I might go with him to his evening service at Taddington, up one of the loveliest dales in Derbyshire. The service was held in a tiny Methodist Chapel in this small hamlet. The congregation consisted of eight people, including my father and myself. The building was lit by three oil lamps, one of which flickered and then went out (I can almost smell the paraffin as I write!). I was interested in the little organ, which seemed all tied up with string and wire. The organist had a loud, harsh voice, the like of which I had not heard before or since; he just roared when he had to bridge an awkward gap caused by one of the wind pedals failing to work properly. Such an ordinary service, or so it seemed, in every way; yet it became for me the most important service I should ever attend.

At the end of his sermon, my father in the words of John Wesley 'offered them Christ' and I found myself, with trembling knees standing on my feet, as the outward sign of an inward decision to receive the new life in Christ and to find the power to overcome temptation and the experience of the forgiveness of sin. I never forgot the burning-heart experience – which Wesley knew when, as he wrote: 'I felt I did trust in Christ, Christ alone for salvation' – which was mine as we travelled home that night.

What changes have taken place since those Bakewell days

as the result of two World Wars, and the rapid advances of
scientific discovery and technology. Some, but not all, have
been for the better; in many ways we have witnessed real
improvement. Here is a recollection which makes the point.
When King George V was crowned in 1911, the Town
Council desired to hold a service on Sunday afternoon in the
Market Square. The Vicar (then Suffragan Bishop of Derby)
and the Free Church ministers, consisting of my father and
the Congregational minister, were invited to take part. The
Vicar absolutely refused to stand on the same platform as my
father, whom he described as a dissenter in most dis-
courteous, if not rude, fashion. He thereupon arranged a
service in the Parish Church for the same hour.

Many years later I received a letter from the Headmaster
of Lady Manners Grammar School saying that he had discovered that I was an 'old boy', and inviting me to present
the prizes and make the speech. He said it was the custom
to have a service in the Parish Church at 11.0 a.m. – the
prizegiving being in the afternoon – for parents, staff and
scholars, and asking me to be the preacher, added that this
invitation had the warmest support of the present Vicar. I
was led to the pulpit in due course for the sermon, and as I
mounted the pulpit steps, I thought I could hear the sound
of my father's voice from heaven, saying 'Hallelujah'!

Finally, it was at Bakewell that I began to dream of becoming a preacher – a desire I first shared with my mother.
My father's example, my conversion, my home in which
preachers were often entertained, and other ministries of the
Holy Spirit, were used to foster this ambition, which at first
seemed a vain hope, mainly because of my shy and very
nervous temperament.

3

Lover of Soil

'When tillage begins, other arts follow. The farmers, therefore, are the founders of human civilization'.
David Webster: 'Remarks on Agriculture'

We moved from Bakewell to Norton-on-Tees and it was here that two vital decisions were made which have influenced my whole life, namely my choice of a career, and my beginning to preach.

I have often said that in all my public speaking I have had but one theme: 'The Cultivation of the Soul and of the Soil'. What finer theme could a man have, the material and the spiritual which in our creation God made one? Voltaire once said: 'The best thing you have to do on earth is to cultivate it', but that is not the whole truth. 'Man shall not live by bread alone', said Jesus, and the emphasis should be on the word 'alone'. He cannot live without food for the body, and the Kingdom of God is concerned with men's bodies as well as their souls.

From early boyhood days, I wanted to be a farmer, and found much pleasure in the illustrations, if unable to follow some of the text, in the weekly paper known as *The Farmer and Stockbreeder*. I also visited my grandfather's farm at Robin Hood's Well and made lists and drawings of stock both live and 'dead' (as machines and implements were called) for the farm I hoped some day to occupy, giving it the significant name of 'Providence Farm'. Arrangements were made when we came to Norton-on-Tees for me to go as a farm pupil on the farm of Mr. John Hall, Middlefield

House, Stockton-on-Tees. The farm lay two or three miles from the Manse, and for a year I rose before 6 o'clock in the morning to cycle to the farm in time to begin work with the resident staff, finishing work (except in haytime and harvest) at 5.0 p.m. I was never late during my twelve months at Middlefield, though one morning it was a near thing.

My father, having called me, did not hear me leave the house, but discovered that I had fallen asleep on my knees saying my prayers! On arrival home in the evening, after my meal I was so tired that in a few minutes I would doze off. I learned from first hand experience not to expect much reading or study from a farm student, if he is at work in the open air all day.

At the end of the year I was encouraged to look round for a small farm which I might rent and, with the help of Mr. Hall as consultant, farm for myself. Looking back now, I realize that it was a foolish idea for one so young and with such limited experience. The fact was, though I did not confess it, I did not feel confident of making a success of a farming venture then, and although values of stock, machinery, rent, etc., were so much lower than now, felt nervous about jeopardizing the whole of the family capital. During this period of uncertainty, my father saw advertised in a Durham County newspaper a course of study for young agriculturists at the Agricultural Department of Armstrong College (then a unit of Durham University), Newcastle upon Tyne. The course was for six weeks only, fees paid and £1.00 a week given for maintenance. Hence my arrival as a "Squeaker" (as the Six Weekers were nicknamed) at the College, and at a very small attic bed-sitting room in lodgings in keeping with my modest maintenance allowance. In the first fortnight I learned that a scholarship covering three years was awarded to the student scoring highest marks in the examination held at the end of the course. I wrote and told my father about it. My father's reply was terse and to the point: 'Take your jacket off to it and have a go.'

Coming out of the examination room after tackling a rather difficult paper I met another Squeaker.

'How did you get on?' he asked.

'Not too well, I'm afraid', I replied. 'What about you?'

'Oh, I was all right with my crib. Didn't you have one?'

He then showed me a thin, neatly folded piece of paper carrying in the smallest writing percentages and other references. It was my first experience of cheating of this kind. Since then I must have invigilated scores of times at examinations, but I have never detected a similar example. Seeing this crib was shattering to my morale. It was therefore a happy surprise when I was awarded the scholarship.

The College at which I was a student for the next three years has had four different names. It began as the (Durham) College of Physical Science (1871-1905), then was re-named Armstrong College (University of Durham), though Durham is 13 miles from Newcastle; it was re-named King's College (1937-63), still remaining part of the University of Durham. From 1963 onwards it has formed the University of Newcastle. Agriculture was a Department under the College name, but is now known as the University School of Agriculture. The motto of Armstrong College, which I noted on beginning my studies, was 'Mens agitat molem' – 'Mind moves mass'.

The new scholarship again provided for all tuition and examination fees to be paid by Durham County Council with £1.00 a week maintenance during term time. I went back to my previous lodgings and arranged terms of 13/- a week for bed and breakfast and light (the right word!) supper. Most days I visited the same cafe at mid-day and rang the changes between tuna tinned fish and sausage. Thus with £5 on my birthday from Father and Mother and £5 from the same source at Christmas, together with earnings during my vacations, I managed to keep going, but not without strict economy. In my third and final year my college friend, Harry Robinson (later to become Dean of the Faculty of Agriculture, Nottingham University), encouraged me to see his landlady, and having now a small financial reserve, I accepted his suggestion. She showed me a lovely clean, single bedroom (what a contrast to my attic!) and asked me if I would share Mr. Robinson's sitting room downstairs, bed, breakfast and a cooked evening meal, for £1.00 a week. I needed no persuasion.

My agricultural career, arduous, though always interesting, was to occupy the next fifty years. On my first summer vacation I was offered by my Professor the temporary post of Record Keeper of the Northumberland Experimental Station at Cockle Park. This is situated nineteen miles from Newcastle, a mile or two from the A1, three miles north of Morpeth. The farmhouse was then an old Pele Tower, walls several feet in width, yet cold and damp. Here I had a bedroom at the top of the Tower, which stands completely exposed to the North East winds, being six miles from the sea coast as the crow flies. I remember my first night because of an experience of home-sickness which made sleep impossible. In the middle of the night, I got out of bed and looked out of the window, feeling desperately lonely and dispirited. The night sky was full of bright stars, and suddenly some words I had learned as a boy came to mind:

'Look up, look up, the stars above
Remind you of His ceaseless love'.

I recalled for a few moments how God had blessed me through the years by the love which never fails and I knew in that somewhat cheerless room the presence of 'the Loved

Unseen'. It was enough. I got back into bed and slept soundly.

My salary was at the rate of £75 per annum, out of which I had to pay the Farm Manager 17/6 weekly for board and lodging and once a fortnight 2/6 for laundry work done by one of the cottagers on the farm. My duties were to keep all records of experiments, measuring out plots, weighing fertilizers for them, and the crops harvested, sending in reports to the College at Newcastle. Every day at 9.0 a.m. and 9.0 p.m. I took the records of the Weather Station – that is seven days a week – which were tabulated in a weekly report and a still more detailed one at the end of the month – both of which were posted to the Meteorological Office in London, as well as copies to Newcastle. I had, therefore, an early introduction in my academic career to one of the most famed experimental farms – especially known for its improvement of grassland trials. I never dreamed that one day I should become mainly responsible for its scientific direction (1947-1955) and that I should write the history of the farm and its experiments from 1896 to 1956.*

This experience during 1916 proved invaluable, for not only various organized parties of students, but of farmers from different parts of the country, as well as scientists and also visitors from other countries, visited the station. The Record Keeper had on such occasions not only to assist the Director or College staff demonstrator in explaining the trials and interpreting the results, but from time to time had to accept responsibility for showing visitors round.

On my return to the College, I was asked to postpone my third and final year to enable me to assist with the teaching, owing to a shortage of staff on account of the First World War. This I agreed to do at the request of Professor D. A. Gilchrist.

*Cockle Park Farm – University of Durham Publications – pub., Oxford University Press.

'I am going to pay you more than I ever paid any previous assistant of mine,' he announced. My £75 per annum began to look very small and I immediately thought of wonderful possibilities. Then he said with great deliberation:

'Your salary will be at the rate of £100 a year!' Well, at least I had got into three figures.

It is now time to explain how it was that I happened to be available for this position and not in the army. I offered for military service five times in all and each time was turned down. On the final occasion I was classified C3 and informed by the presiding medical office I would do better service for my country working in agriculture. I inquired further and was informed that I had been rejected because of a heart murmur. This disconcerted me so much at this early juncture in my career that I consulted privately the well known consultant, Sir David Drummond, one time President of the College of Newcastle Medical School. He confirmed the diagnosis, but added this reassurance:

'Try to forget about it except for remembering never to run after a train or tram or rush upstairs.'

Due to my upbringing, I made this handicap a matter of prayer. Many years passed and along with other members of the teaching staff I was given the opportunity to change my pension annuity into a life assurance policy. This involved a medical examination. When asked if I had any health problems, I mentioned my heart murmur. The doctor placed a chair in front of me.

'Get up and down on that chair' – if I remember correctly – 'fifteen or twenty times quickly'. Then immediately he applied the stethoscope. 'Well', he said, 'you may have had a heart murmur, but there is no trace of it now.' There was no difficulty about the insurance policy, and I did not forget to offer my prayer of thanksgiving that evening.

For most of my agricultural life, I have been concerned

with food production – in two World Wars and with the ever-enlarging knowledge of the need of hungry people in the world. My teaching subject throughout was Crop Husbandry, but I always sought to recognize its close relationship to Animal Husbandry, both of which are dependent upon the third factor in this God-created trinity, namely the Soil.

I was appointed lecturer in agriculture on probation in 1917 in what is now the University of Newcastle. As a University teacher, I loved my work and for forty years served as lecturer and then Professor of Agriculture (1948-57) in my Alma Mater. I was once asked by my greatest friend if my preaching helped my lecturing, and I replied that it did. For both I had framed three guiding principles: (1) to be interesting, (2) to be informative, and (3) to be inspiring. This is not mere alliteration. The last mentioned is perhaps the most difficult to describe. If you don't interest people, they won't listen, and your lecture ought to leave a student with information in his mind and note-book worth remembering. But to inspire is to make him feel he himself can make something of what he has learned in the fulfilment of his life's ambitions.

After some years of teaching, a past student, who had made rapid progress in his career, came to tell me of an appointment he had just accepted under the newly formed Sulphate of Ammonia Federation to organize an agricultural advisory service, and he sought to persuade me to join him as deputy. He offered to treble my present salary (then about £250), and said that together we could develop an organization covering the country. I took a week-end prayerfully to consider it, and then declined his kind offer. His forecast of the future was quite correct for, not very long after that, the Federation became part of the newly formed combine known as Imperial Chemical Industries, and my past student's salary advanced into the thousands. I have never regretted the decision, for to me nothing is quite so wonderful as doing something, however small it may seem, to fashion the character and assist in the equipment of young people training for a career.

In addition to my activities within the Department of Agriculture I had to undertake 'outside' lectures to farmers and later Young Farmers' Clubs and other such rural institutions. The first of these, I well remember, was at a place called Cold Heseldon in County Durham, where I lectured on 'Manures and Manuring'. I confess I felt very young and inexperienced in such an adult audience, but I cannot believe that I inspired much enthusiasm. I well remember the question which seemed the most imporant to them. It was of few words: 'Will it pay?' I was to meet this question time and time again down the years, so I was early introduced to the subject of Agricultural economics – a subject then not included as such in the agricultural curriculum.

I became intensely interested in the experiments in the improvement of poor grassland conducted at Cockle Park (the Northumberland Agricultural Experimental Station) and, in external lectures, visits to farms, and demonstrations to visiting parties of farmers to the Experimental Station, preached with enthusiasm the virtues of basic slag for the improvement of old permanent grass and the inclusion of wild white clover seed supported by basic slag treatment of the soil in seeding down new grassland. These were the outstanding discoveries, with all their attendant questions of management of grazing, of Sir William Somerville, the first Scientific Director of Cockle Park, Sir Thomas Middleton who succeeded him, and my own Professor, namely Professor Gilchrist (who deserved as much as his predecessors a knighthood, but never received it), who followed Middleton and was Director for twenty-five years. No work in the history of agricultural scientific development as applied to the land, I judge, has been of more value than that accomplished by these three men. 'Basic Slag and Wild White Clover' became a slogan or motto for the Agricultural Department of what was then known as Armstrong College.

Although I was interested in all farm crops – because I taught mainly Crop Husbandry – it was natural, I suppose, that I became best known for my efforts to improve grassland and in particular my contribution to the spread and acceptance of the principle that grass was just as much a farm crop as barley or turnips – a principle which was either neglected or ignored by a large majority of farmers when I began my career. Grass was regarded as what nature provided and the sole fertilization consisted of animal droppings with a very limited use of lime, and that happened on many farms where arable crops received elaborate cultivation and often generous use of artificial as well as natural manure. I used to teach and preach that grass, *like any other crop*, required cultivation, fertilization and efficient harvesting or utilization. Today grass has very largely taken the place of the root crop as the restorative pivot crop of fertility to be used to produce the exhaustive corn crops. In its way this change in the general attitude of the farmer to grass is one of the most revolutionary and far-reaching changes in farm production in the agricultural history of the country and there are no better farmers anywhere in the world than in Britain.

In 1939, I was seconded by the University to the Government as Chief Technical Adviser to the Northumberland War Agricultural Executive Committee, and this position I held until a year after the war finished in 1945. I always think of these years as the most strenuous, and most rewarding, of my agricultural career. I had a twofold understanding with the Committee, that I would not do advisory work on Sundays, and that I would visit farmers purely as an adviser and not to give official orders or report any misdoings. I was desirous of winning their confidence as a friend who wanted to co-operate and not compel in seeking improvement, and I cannot help feeling this policy was justified.

With 4,100 farmers in the country, I realized that alone I could not hope to meet more than a fraction of the need. During the day before a conference with 'high-ups' in the Ministry of Agriculture, I drew up an advisory scheme for Northumberland providing for assistants stationed at strategic points in the county, each having a thousand or so farmers under his care, myself continuing at the Department of Agriculture at King's College, Newcastle, and free to visit any district or farm.

The senior Ministry of Agriculture member presided next day and began by saying: 'I should explain that we have convened this Conference to get your ideas and discuss how best we can help you with them.' He looked appealingly to Major Rea, Chairman of the War Agricultural Committee. He replied: 'I think our Chief Technical Officer could do this best.' Whereupon I handed a copy of my scheme to the presiding official and proceeded to go over it point by point. Later, Major Rea kindly spoke to me privately.

'Well, Pawson, you've certainly put Northumberland on the map of Whitehall.'

I confess to being pleased with the result of my anticipating what ought to be the purpose of this Conference.

I was naturally not displeased to find that, when the Luxmore Committee Report during the war resulted in the formation of the National Agricultural Advisory Service (N.A.A.S.) at a later date, some of its features bore a close resemblance to my humble report – for example, District Advisory Officers with 1,000 farmers or suitable areas on an acreage basis.

I attribute to this minor success an invitation from the

Ministry of Agriculture some time later to attend a large Press Conference at Whitehall to form one of a team of four, with Donald McCulloch of B.B.C. fame as Question Master, dealing with the food production campaign. At the end of the war, when to my complete surprise I was awarded the M.B.E. (compared with today very few such decorations were given for those who had been engaged in this particular kind of war-time work), in retrospect I thought these early experiences had been steps towards this recognition.

It would require another book to attempt to do justice to the interest and worthwhileness of this war-time work, but one or two illustrations will be of interest. 1940 was the epoch-making year of the Farm Survey – never since Doomsday Book had such an examination of all the farms in the country been made, and it was, of course, more extensive than the Doomsday Book. It was a stroke of genius to enlist the aid of the farmers in this great national effort to produce more home-grown foods. Two farmers visited each farm and graded the same as follows:

Grade A   Management first class.

Grade B   Good but with room for improvement.

Grade C   Poor, subdivided as follows:
   because of
   (a) shortage of capital resources;
   (b) an inherently poor farm of very limited potential;
   (c) poor, inefficient farmer.

All these particulars for every farm in each county were available to the War Agricultural Executive and local District Committees. Naturally a technical adviser gave most attention to B and particularly C farms, although this did not preclude visits to A farms and, as all who have experience of agricultural advisory work know, it is usually the better or best farmers who are keenest on new ideas and the most ready to accept suggestions.

My first job for the County Committee was to investigate all the reported failures in establishing satisfactory wheat plants. It should be remembered that the overall objective of the Government was to ensure increased arable crops from ploughing out grassland. Every county received the figure for the desired quota and every farm, if at all practicable, was expected to provide an acreage for this purpose. Shortage of implements and experience of ploughing out and managing new arable land were real difficulties, and many had to rely on contractors (who in consequence developed a service and played an increasingly important part in the war effort). I discovered several failures were to be found on outlying farms where individual acreages were not large and all the work of preparation of the land and sowing had to be done by contract. Naturally there was a tendency in some cases to leave such to be done when the larger contracts had been completed and, when their turn came, to do everything in the shortest possible time – in a few hours or at most a day or two.

Now I remembered an old saying that 'wheat likes a stale furrow' which is best translated 'a firm settled seed-bed'. In practice this means that in walking over a wheat sown field there should be no occasional sinking in of the heel indicating an air pocket under the ploughed furrow, otherwise the young wheat plants, failing to become deep rooted, will especially in spring dry out and die. Very thorough disc harrowing and sometimes supplementary heavy rolling secures a uniformly firm seed-bed, but this takes time and it is work which cannot be rushed. When the wheat (if it had been autumn sown) had failed completely – though often good recovery can be obtained by Cambridge roller and harrow in spring –

I usually advised an alternate crop like spring barley.

Very early in this work of war-time advising, I arranged with my colleague and friend in the College, Dr. Brynmor Thomas, our Advisory Chemist, to analyse samples of soil from fields scheduled to be ploughed out. The report sent without prejudice to the farmer indicated any deficiencies (lime and phosphate being the most common) and suggested dressing of fertilizers. In as many cases as possible I took the report to the farmer for personal interpretation and further advice if needed. This was so much appreciated that further samples were often requested and in some cases to include every field on the farm.

One instance may be quoted of a farm in the last men-tioned category. Meeting the farm manager with the report, I said everything seemed straightforward but in going round with him there was one field that I particularly wished to see, where the sampling was given in reports A and B.

'Well, that's all one field', he replied, and repeated it more than once. Finally some distance before reaching the field in qustion, we stopped at a gate.

'There must be some marked difference', I said, 'between two portions of this field when one shows a good phosphate figure but low in potash and the other low in phosphate but better in potash. Are you sure the whole field has received the same treatment?'

"Well, as a matter of fact, we cut the most convenient part of it for hay every year and just graze the remaining portion'.

'Now', I said, 'I've got the explanation. The chemist who analysed the samples has never seen the field and neither have I, but the report confirms the accuracy of the test. I suppose you seldom give this field a dressing of farmyard manure, with all the demand for manure on your arable

land, and from the map I can see how outlying and incon-
venient is this field for such manuring.'

'You are quite right', he said. 'it never sees the dung cart,
but mind you, I gave it in recent years a very good dressing
of basic slag (phosphates).'

'All of it?' I inquired.

'Oh no, just the area from which we take the hay.'

I then explained to him that every load of hay taken from
the field removed potash from the soil, but that practically all
the potash taken by a grazing animal in the herbage is returned in the solid and liquid extract – hence the report was
a true reflection of the management.

It may be of interest to non-agricultural readers to know
why the ploughing out of grassland for other cropping was
the main objective in bringing about increased production for
our war-time needs. When conditions permit there can be no
argument against ploughing out poor grassland to produce a
new sward. The old saying, 'To make a pasture will break a
man, to break a pasture will make a man', was true when
corn prices were good and when knowledge of seed mixtures
for establishing a turf was deficient, because it then took
years of competition between sown grass-seed and weeds to
settle down to something like a pasture. Professor Gilchrist's
simplified, balanced 'Cockle Park mixture' backed up by a
dressing of basic slag to encourage the rapid spread and complete undercovering of the herbage with wild white clover
(to suppress weeds) rendered the old saying obsolete. Cockle
Park seeds mixture became the best known from John o'
Groats to Land's End because of this success.

I always think of this war period as an agricultural adviser's most challenging opportunity. For one thing, there
was a wonderful, dynamic spirit of co-operation and enterprise. In farmers' discussion meetings and demonstrations on
farms, enthusiastic audiences of 100 or more were not

uncommon, and a magnificent team spirit prevailed between representatives of both practice and science. Alas, the patriotism of war does not always result in a patriotism of peace, though the need remains the same.

In another way the war provided the realization of an agricultural adviser's dream. One example again must suffice. Every effort was made by persuasion and advice to increase the productivity of C farms and it was not long before orders to plough out grassland were the rule for all classes of farmers. Despite orders and persuasion there were still some C Farmers who failed to achieve the standard judged possible and these were taken over by the Executive Committee to whom had been given as a war-time regulation the power to dispossess an unsatisfactory farmer. The farmer in question was given a chance to state his difficulties and warned of the consequences if improvement was not forthcoming. It speaks much for the high standard of farming in Northumberland that the number of farmers thus dispossessed could be counted – if my memory is correct – on two hands.

Hole Row farm, in the south-west of the country, was one of such farms which illustrates what can be done when all the resources of known agricultural science (always an increasing knowledge as research continues) and sound practice are applied. Several local farmers were pessimistic about what could be done to improve it. I had all the fields tested for plant food deficiencies and I obtained an independent valuer's report on the farm's condition. We then carried out drainage, fencing, manurial treatment, cropping and cultivation requirements, including also certain building improvements. At that time money was secondary to improvement in production, or as I heard it said, 'If Hitler starves us out and gets to the Bank of England, our gold reserves will not save us.' Few people realized that in the First World War we came within a week-end supply of food reserves owing to the submarine offensive on our shipping. So we put in all we could at Hole Row in twelve months.

The outcome was a source of great satisfaction. In due course I arranged a demonstration for farmers which aroused great interest and was very well attended. Taking the party round the farm was one of the most pleasurable days I have ever spent. My war-time experiences confirmed a long held conviction that if the results of our present knowledge of scientific agriculture were fully applied, we could go a long way to solving the problem of a hungry world, but more on that question in later chapters.

Suffice it to say, at this point, that I became firmly convinced during these war years that we had farmers in this country second to none in the world. As the result of the Food Production Campaign, production was increased by the end of the war by about 70%. To me, one of the most praiseworthy things I noted prevailing among so many of the farmers with whom I had contact was not so much their fear that the Government would let them down, as happened after the First World War, as that they might impair the cropping of their land for the future by excessive emphasis on intensive corn cropping. This is an instinctive feeling of a good husbandman, the care of the soil under his stewardship.

I hope the experiences recorded will not be regarded as a mere success story; I have made mistakes and experienced failures and disappointments. If this book does not contain a description of 'warts and all', I am nevertheless aware of them. My dominant ambition throughout was to serve God and my fellow men in the two spheres of religion and agriculture.

4

Research

'Nothing has such power to broaden the mind as the ability to investigate systematically and truly all that comes under thy observation in life.'

Marcus Aurelius in 'Meditations'.

In my earlier years on the college staff I formed the opinion that the teacher is not well balanced who does not undertake some original research. Admittedly his time-table limits his opportunity for research, and he cannot compete with the full-time research worker. Nevertheless, it is better to try and combine, in whatever way is possible, teaching and research.

Very early in my teaching career, I mapped out a subject for research and had the temerity to submit it to Sir John Russell, the Director of the oldest and most famed agricultural experimental centre in the world at Rothamsted (Herts). His major criticism was that I had taken too large a canvas. I should confine my investigation, for example, to livestock and why black cattle, for instance, were found in Scotland and the red cattle by the Celts in the West of England and Wales. I marvel that this great, well-known scientist should go to such trouble over an unknown young man, but Sir John was an example of the spirit I have found in truly great men throughout my life, humble enough to make ordinary juniors believe in themselves. He was Director of Rothamsted for over 30 years until his retirement at the age of 70 in 1943.

Despite the encouragement Sir John gave me, I regret to

say I never accomplished it to my satisfaction, but I was glad I was able to show my appreciation of him and his fine work by supporting through Press articles in the North and in other ways the national appeal that was made to purchase the Rothamsted estate and farm, to save it from being lost to agriculture because of building developments and urban planners. My last personal contact with him was in Manchester, where he delivered the Beckley Lecture in July, 1955, subsequently published by Epworth Press, entitled 'Science and Modern Life'.

In those earlier years, realizing that my training and experience had been limited to North-East England, I began to take every possible opportunity of observing first-hand farming in other areas in Great Britain. To this day I still receive bulletins and reports from several centres as a result.

For my M.Sc. degree, which I obtained in 1946, I presented a thesis on 'The Meadow Hay Crop' with special reference to its production on Hill Farms. This arose out of a challenge put by a questioner after a lecture I gave at Blanchland on the management of grassland. Hay is *the* crop on a hill farm, and I tried to show that by correct fertilization the yield and quality could be improved, using the results of Palace Leas Meadow Hay trials at Cockle Park, where double the untreated crop and much better feeding quality had been obtained, but illustrating as well how needful it is to discriminate in the use of fertilizers.

My questioner said these results were useless to them and inquired when the artifical fertilizers were applied and how long was the field shut off from stock grazing to grow the crop. I replied that we cleared the land of stock in March, and the nitrogenous part of the fertilizer treatment was then given. Immediately, I sensed a gleam of triumph in my critic.

"We lamb our ewes in April and early May, and the fields cannot be cleared of stock until then, so that's that.'

I took up the challenge and asked if any farmer present would allow me to lay down plots on two of his meadows to demonstrate my faith that it could be done. Most hill farmers at that time, years before the Second World War, relied on what little farmyard manure they could scrape together, very limited in quantity and invariably depleted in nitrogen, which drained away from the heap exposed to the winter rains. I subsequently had analysed a sample of such manure and found it contained a greatly reduced nitrogen control when compared with such manure under cover, in which the urine is conserved, which urine is roughly two-thirds of the value of farmyard manure.

A farmer offered two of his meadows and subsequently I found two other hill farms in other districts (two meadows on each farm), one farm of very high class fertility (that of a man who in the years that followed became a dear friend after that meeting, namely Mr. Jasper Stephenson M.B.E. of Blanchland), another a farm of medium fertility, and one at the bottom of the scale. For the last named, the shepherd said the hay crop was usually so poor 'in a windy hay time it blew into the next parish'! The results exceeded our highest hopes. The late application of the fertilizers which in no way interfered with the usual lambing dates, gave splendid results. For the complete artificial fertilizers the percentage increase for the first three years at Cockle Park was 43%, whilst in the hill farm trials it was 55%. The final report exerted an influence on better treatment of what is called in-bye land on hill farms, namely the enclosed fields, which I was able to carry further during the Second World War, when the plough became more common in use and fields could be re-sown and new grass established.

In July 1923, I paid my first visit to the Rowett Institute, Bucksburn, near Aberdeen, which was largely concerned with a neglected aspect of nutrition for livestock, namely the mineral content of the ration. Anaemia in young pigs, which then accounted for a high mortality, was found to be due to the deficiency in iron. The work at the Rowett Institute later broadened to include and inspire diet survey which led ultimately to free milk at schools for children, a health-giving supplement resulting in the much better nourished children, with which the names of Boyd-Orr* and Walter Elliot (one-time Minister of Agriculture) will always be associated.

Boyd-Orr tried to establish a World Food Board after the Second World War at the International Conference called by the late President Roosevelt, and he was able to get co-operation among the nations to deal with the immediate post-war food crises. But on a permanent basis he failed because, though all other member nations of F.A.O. were willing to co-operate, the then all-powerful Britain and the America (1970) refused to join. But his failure was greater than many men's success, in that some day his vision of food for a hungry world will be realized, and he will come into his own in history's record.

At one stage, the member of the Rowett Institute staff showing me round was called away for some important telephone call, and he left me with the head pigman, who showed me some new piggeries recently completed and used for the first time for an experiment. My guide showed me these three new yards, then empty, but which only a few days earlier had housed three lots of pigs, one lot fed on a lime deficient ration, one lot on a medium lime control ration, and one on a normal ration. He then said: 'You see that heap of builders' lime over there?' pointing to a large dump perhaps fifty yards away.

'Well', he said, 'when we let all the pigs out to drive them

* See the most readable and inspiring autobiography *As I recall it*, Lord Boyd-Orr, published in 1966.

together to a large yard where they are now, believe it or not, sir, the pigs which had been on a no-lime ration dashed across to that heap and started to eat it as you would ice cream, and no amount of stick slapping would drive them off it. After they had had their fill of it they lay on the heap and went off to sleep, and now they appear none the worse for gorging it up.'

Thus was a seed thought put into a new file in my mind under my heading of 'Animal Instinctive Behaviour', which many years later led to another of my research projects.

I was in the company of notable grassland experts when the farmer whose fine grass field we were inspecting said:

'Now can any of you expert gentlemen tell me why, when such a beautiful sward of grasses and clover like this is available, a lamb or ewe will occasionally nibble at the thorn hedge?'

I waited for the greatest authority (as I judged) to answer, and finally he said: 'Curiosity'. I felt it was a totally inadequate reply, and remembered the Rowett incident of the pigs.

The next step was to study the neglected subject in animal nutrition research of the diet of hill ewes. Feeding standards for all other classes of livestock were available, but not for hill ewes. My very able colleague at the University, Dr. Brynmor Thomas, became interested, and in this as well as other subjects we enjoyed a happy and fruitful collaboration. His work on the composition of heather and other hill as well as lowland plants was a splendid contribution to our knowledge of their chemical composition. Samples of heather of known age after burning (the only 'cultivation' of this valuable hill ewe feeding crop) were taken from a farm and analysed. We experimented with the effect of fertilizers, and Thomas carried out exhaustive examination of other plants found on black land (where heather predominates it is called 'black'; when rough grass is dominant with little heather it is described as 'white'). To me, one of the most interesting plants was the draw moss, or cotton grass (*Eriophorum angustifolium*). It disappears if the land is drained, growing best in moist or damp places. In appearance it is like a spring onion and is greatly favoured by the hill ewes, who pull it up and consume it avidly in early spring. On analysis, it was found that the scallion end was particularly rich in phosphate content, and this, with the analysis of young and old heather, with a varying *seasonal* lime content and at best somewhat low in phosphate, led me to think more of how animals seek to adjust deficiencies in their natural diet, and to believe that in improving both the bulk and quality (protein and minerals) of the hill farm hay crop the sheep could be assisted in their diet.

One other illustration must suffice. I was inspecting my plots on one of the hill farm meadows mentioned earlier when the shepherd drew my attention to a plant visible here and there. He drew one out of the ground and said:

'What is this?'

'I don't know, though I am pretty sure it belongs to the thistle family', I replied. 'Let's gather a sample.'

Arriving back at College, I sent half my sample to the Professor of Botany and half to my colleague Dr. Brynmor Thomas, the chemist. I sent to the last named because when I inquired about the shepherd's interest in the plant he told me that when the rams were brought back from the hill (they are turned out to the ewes in November for the breeding period) and brought into this meadow, they go for the plant first of all and eat it to the bone greedily.

The first to reply was the Professor of Botany, who said it was called the Melancholy Thistle (*Circium Heterophyllum*) and it was suggested that it derived its name from a brew made from its leaves as a cure or palliative for depression. It is also of interest to note that it was one of the personal badges of the House of Stewart.

The chemist reported that the figure for the lime content was the largest ever known in his analytical work. Now the rams coming off the hill at a time of the year when the lime content of the heather *was at its lowest* found what they needed in the thistle.

Agricultural research affords one of the most interesting of all subjects, so it seems to me, for investigation. There is full international sharing of the results and, as in the medical world, nothing but good can obtain if the knowledge thus gained is wisely applied for the betterment of mankind.

As a means of placing this chapter in a wider setting I have considered how I would answer the question: 'What in your opinion is the greatest discovery affecting agriculture beneficially and therefore mankind in your life-time?' I have reflected on the amazing developments of mechanization; the wealth of knowledge gained at Rothamsted on plant nutrition; the work on the nutrition of farm animals at Cambridge, the Rowett Institute and elsewhere, and the work of plant breeders in producing varieties of cereals and forage plants which when adequately fertilized produce vastly improved yields. I have remembered, too, the pioneer work in improved grassland management of which I had first-hand knowledge.

Yet I think I would single out for my answer the discovery of how to abstract nitrogen from the atmosphere and the development of the synthetic process whereby artificial fertilizers are now produced supplying nitrogen either alone, or more commonly in combination with other plant food requirements known as 'compounds'.

The artificial manure industry now producing in such vast quantities for export and home use had its birth in the work of the country squire, John Lawes, who at Rothamsted in

The Author
and his wife.

A
Ruby
Wedding
Family
Group,
including
the nine
grandchildren.

Tower at Cockle Park, the Northumberland Agricultural Experimental Station, with which the Author had long association.

Newspaper announcement!

Original members of the Author's Tuesday Class-meeting.

1842 produced super-phosphate by treating in a crucible a small amount of bone material with sulphuric acid, which process he patented and in 1875 his manure business was sold for £300,000 of which £100,000 was used to maintain his work at Rothamstead under the Lawes Agricultural Trust.

The most important plant food constituents are nitrogen, phosphate and potash together with the soil base of lime. These are the 'Big Four' in fertilization. Nitrogen's chief effect is on the leaves and stem or green parts above ground and the leaf is the laboratory of the plant where protein is produced from the nitrogen absorbed by the roots (the mouths of the plant). Sir William Crookes, in his Presidential address to the British Association in 1898, forecasted a shortage of world nitrogen by the '30s of the present century. 'Necessity is the mother of invention', hence the attention of scientists given to that unlimited amount of nitrogen in the atmosphere (4/5 nitrogen, 1/5 oxygen) and their discovery that it could be taken from the air and fixed in a form which could be transported and applied to the soil. The synthetic process of fertilizers carried this successful method of doing so still further.

When I lived at Norton-on-Tees I used to go to preach on Sundays in our small Chapel in the village of Billingham, just a mile or two away. Today it is a large town dominated by the huge towers and works of I.C.I. which, like the fellow giant enterprises of Fison's, produce those synthetic fertilizers and obtain from the air vast quantities of nitrogen to stimulate grass and cereal growth, both here and overseas. Thus tremendous increases in production of crop are possible in under-developed areas of the world and for that matter here in this country, wherever the full potential has not yet been attained. I often think in association with the discovery or exploitation of this new source of nitrogen of the words in Shakespeare's *Hamlet* (Act III, Scene 2): 'I

c

eat the air promise crammed' (or 'stuffed with promises'), for that is just what we do when we eat our daily bread produced from the wheat which is so dependent upon an ample supply of nitrogen.

Other exciting discoveries of the kind are sure to come. I tasted, not long ago, a protein meal extracted from oil, and there will also be further developments of synthetic food products and from the sea flora. Mankind continues to owe more than can be described to agricultural and other branches of research. Our abiding need is the wise use of all such discoveries for the blessing not the curse of the human beings who make up our world, ever remembering a favourite saying in my home, namely: 'People are more important than things'.

When I cast my mind over the subject of this chapter and my own minor contributions, I always think of those following who carry on the good work others have to lay down. To have done anything at all to encourage these is truly satisfying to a retired college don like myself.

5
Lover of Souls

'I preached as never sure to preach again and as a dying man
to dying men.'
Richard Baxter

During the period when we lived at Norton-on-Tees, I
began to preach – a momentous happening in my life – resulting in increasing joy which after fifty-six years of preaching is greater today than ever. I do not think there is any joy
to be experienced on earth greater that that of proclaiming
what the Bible describes as 'glad tidings of good things'. Although then, and to this day, I have felt handicapped by
extreme nervousness before a service, I cannot be sufficiently
thankful for the call to preach and the signs God has granted
me confirming its validity. For the benefit of those who experience the same difficulty, a brief mention of the action I
adopt might be helpful. Just before the service I seek to
concentrate my thoughts on God and the needs of the people
for whom He has called me to be a channel of blessing. Once
in the pulpit I deliberately relax my body physically in the
opening hymn if I feel excessive tension.

Another physical defect might have put at risk my longing
to preach. In 1920, I began to experience difficulty in finishing my words and sentences. A curious click in my speech
as I lectured began to embarrass me, so I made an appointment with a Newcastle throat specialist. A growth between the vocal chords prevented them from closing and he
advised an immediate operation. The surgeon was able to
inform me that the growth was non-malignant, but that I

must have a course of voice production to get the vocal chords functioning normally again. I shall always be grateful to the late Mr. George Dodds, a teacher of singing in great demand in Newcastle. The gist of his teaching was to throw the voice forward so that you felt you were speaking from the front of the mouth and *not* from the throat, as one is prone to do especially when tired. He insisted that there was never any need for a parson's tired or hoarse voice on a Monday!

Nine years later, in 1929, I took advantage of the offer of a free medical examination – hitherto ignored – attached to a small life insurance. Almost casually, the doctor remarked: 'Do you smoke?' 'Yes', I said. 'What's wrong?'

'There's a slight inflammation in the throat which I think your cigarette smoking may aggravate; but nothing to worry about.

After a considerable struggle I asked for strength to do what I felt was God's will for me in the matter. At the end of a month, I felt there was no need to begin again and have therefore been a non-smoker for more than forty years.

In 1965 I ran into further trouble with my voice and in due course my throat was again very carefully examined.

'Do you redden quickly in the sun?'

'Yes', I replied, 'all too quickly'.

'I have to tell you,' he then said, 'that your throat is chronically inflamed and I can do nothing about it. Above all else, don't retire to a hot country like South Africa or Australia or it would probably be cancer of the throat in a few months.'

He then offered me a reprint from the Journal of Laryngology and Otology (October 1964) which bore the title *A Hoarse Voice and a Red Face*. I was interested to read the conclusion that all likely irritants should be avoided. 'This

entails the abstinence from all types of smoking and excessive intake of alcohol and other vasodilators.'

The doctor's final word arose out of my earlier account, at
his request, of the history of any previous trouble, and in
particular the insurance doctor's advice. 'How wise he was
to advise you as he did. My own judgement is that had
you not followed his advice, you would not have been con-
sulting me today'.

Standing in the queue waiting for the bus to take me
home, I saw a man quite near to me with the reddest face I
can ever remember seeing. I resisted the temptation – not
without difficulty – of asking a complete stranger whether he
suffered from a hoarse voice!

I took my first service in a tiny chapel a mile or two from
my home, at a place called Norton Junction – this building
was on railway property, quite close to a railway line.
There was just a handful of people present, but they were
sympathetic and kind. I had copious notes and got lost in the
middle of my sermon but managed to make my way to the
end in reasonable time. In contrast, my father, who for a
week or two preached his first sermon to the gas lamps on his
way home from work, when it came to the service, had the
Prodigal Son into the far country, feeding the swine and
back home again in three minutes! He told me he was never
sure as to whether he or the prodigal son was the more
exhausted. My own subject was: 'God's Pedestrian', and the
text: 'Enoch walked with God: and he was not; for God took
him'. Many years later, when my mother went to heaven, as
the eldest son I had to go through her papers and private
belongings and in so doing, I discovered the notes of my first
sermon. I never remember giving them to her, but she had
kept them, such is a mother's love. Actually, though some
preachers feel it is better to destroy notes of old sermons, I
have retained mine and find it interesting to trace the

development of my theological knowledge, though I marvel at the tolerance and patience of congregations, especially in my earlier years.

I remember a warning given to me by a retired Methodist minister, to whom I went with unconcealed enthusiasm to tell him I was now on the way to becoming a local preacher. I expected him to receive the news with pleasure and commendation.

'And now your troubles begin, Cecil.'

I was completely taken aback. I looked the dismay I felt.

'What I mean is', he went on, 'that you will find how difficult it is for you to know where to draw the line between your church and preaching work, and your daily job.' How right he was! Every week until my retirement in 1957, I have prayed for the right answer to this persistent question.

One example dates from my appointment as lecturer on probation in agriculture in 1917. There is, of course, no 'clocking in' or prescribed hours of work for University teachers and research workers, but I always refused any invitations to meetings associated with church or similar organizations until after 5.0 p.m. on weeknights. Since 1957 I have been free from this dual concern, though in deciding between the various opportunities of service I still use the daily prayer: 'Lord, what wilt Thou have me to do?' The whole point was that if I was not at my best in my daily work, I would fail as a Christian in the most important sphere of Christian witness.

It is perhaps not altogether surprising that I should have given thought to the possibility of the full-time ministry. I thought that if God's call became clear and the way opened I would like to go to Cambridge to take a degree before seeking acceptance for the ministry and entry to one of our

Methodist ministerial training colleges; and to that end I
wrote for particulars to the University there. The door, however, did not open owing to a family circumstance, which
left several questions not yet fully answered, which some day
I shall understand. When I retired at sixty, my dear friend,
the Rev. Dr. Leslie Weatherhead, wrote me a very loving,
persuasive letter suggesting that under the new conditions in
Methodism for accepting older men into the ministry, I
should now offer myself and promising his support. Another
great friend, the Rev. Dr. Harold Roberts, indicated that if I
thus decided he would do the same, but after renewed
prayer on the question, I became sure it was not God's will
for me.

My very close friend, the Rev. Dr. W. E. Sangster, once
raised the question with me and ended by declaring that I
should never harbour any feelings of regret.

'Doors of witness are open to you that are denied to me,
greatly as I love the full time ministry. They can never say',
he went on, 'that you get your living by professing Christianity and wearing your collar the other way round!' His
conversation, I recall, was both a challenge and a comfort,
for I confess to occasional twinges of longing when talking
and praying with young men – some of whom are my
'sons in the Gospel' before they go off to college as accepted candidates for the ministry.

I have had opportunities entirely unsought of conducting
most services a fully ordained Minister is called upon to conduct regularly. These include Holy Communion at Baptist
Churches, Independent Missions, and assisting the minister
in them at Christian Conferences and Retreats at which I
have been the speaker. By special request of the family, I
took the funeral service of a very great friend at Colvend
Parish Church of Scotland with the full blessing of the Minister. The address was given in the house, only the men, with

their black draped hats accompanying me to the church-yard. I rode in a coach with some of the elders for quite a distance and no one spoke, which in a sense might be considered fitting. Then I asked a question and from the conversation that immediately followed and continued I gained the impression that, as with Royalty, until the Minister speaks on such occasions, all remain silent.

Earlier in my preaching vocation I arrived at a Methodist Church in a colliery village in Northumberland to be told that as a matter of urgency I must baptize two babies. The families and many friends and relations had all come – some from a considerable distance – and the steward had just received word that the minister who was to have conducted the baptismal part of the service had suddenly fallen ill. I demurred, and suggested a postponement, but realizing the disappointment and consternation, I agreed to do as the parents desired.

Finally, the wife of a dear friend proved unfaithful to her husband, on one occasion, but confessed immediately to her partner. Both desired, after confession, penitence, reconciliation, and with their young children in mind and heart, to make a new beginning, and begged me to re-marry them, especially as I had been used some years earlier to lead the husband to give his life to Christ. I wrote to Epworth Press (the Methodist Publishing House) for copies of a beautiful service they publish for such circumstances. Then, with my wife as witness, we held the service in the lounge at Over-dale. Suffice it to say the home and family remain beautiful in their Christian witness, and as faithful members of the Church to this day.

It was Richard Baxter – not Charles Haddon Spurgeon, to whom they are sometimes attributed – whose words at the head of this chapter express the essence of evangelical preaching. Preaching is a matter of life and death, and surely the sense of urgency which possessed the early Church in its proclamation of the Gospel largely accounted for its amazing success. On the last night of a week at Hildenborough Hall, the meeting took the form of a Brains Trust with the late Tom Rees as question master. I have forgotten all the questions save one, which has remained an abiding challenge to me. 'If members of the Brains Trust knew they had only one week to live, how would they spend it?' I know that I answered in effect that I would try to tell as many people as possible about Christ. I would still give the same answer if asked the question today, only I would add Charles Wesley's words:

> Happy, if with my latest breath
> I might but gasp His Name;
> Preach Him to all, and cry in death:
> Behold, behold the Lamb!

Soon after I became a local preacher, I was led, so I believed, to make two vows. (1) That I would never make any request regarding my appointments – that is for the Circuit plan of appointments which in Methodism is printed quarterly – and (2) that I would never take expenses for my preaching and other church work, committees and so on. I have managed to keep these two vows all through the years. With regard to the second, when out of my own circuit, I make quite clear to the stewards concerned that I expect them to *offer* expenses, as is the accepted practice, for many of my preacher brethren could not afford to decline this financial assistance. A book or a book token sent very occasionally afterwards has, of course, been gratefully accepted.

One of the most remarkable answers to prayer in my preaching experience is worthy of record. One Sunday morning my wife felt constrained to look in our letter box – a quite unusual action, as we have no delivery on Sundays. She discovered an unstamped envelope and, from the hand-writing, judged it probably to be a request for financial help of some kind and felt inclined not to pass it on to me until I had finished my preaching work for the day. Yet a sense of constraint led her to change her mind. I glanced at it and almost made the same decision to leave it unopened but, as with my wife, later felt that I must open it. It contained a letter from a woman I knew, whose husband often deserted her, pawning things taken from the home for money for his own purposes. Enclosed was a solicitor's demand for payment of a certain sum of money, amounting to some pounds, within two days, otherwise they would take steps to dispose of what she had left of personal possessions. She begged me for help to tide over their financial crisis.

Now it so happened that I had given more financial help during that week than I felt was justified as a married man with a growing family, and I honestly felt – much as I sympathized with the woman – that it would not be right for me to send her this sum in time for Tuesday morning. So in a brief prayer, I asked God to undertake for me in this dilemma. Thereupon *I forgot all about both the woman and letter.*

After the service, several persons kindly came to shake my hand. The last one to approach me was a man.

'I want you to know that I re-dedicated my life to God at the end of your sermon,' he said. Then, apparently quite casually, he added, 'And what you are holding in your hand, God told me to give you as we were singing the last hymn. I do not know for what purpose, but you will be guided.'

He left the church and I opened my hand and unrolled a number of pound notes. I rushed after him and told him that I never accepted a penny for my services. Then I asked him to read the letter and enclosure I had received that morning. He looked the astonishment we both felt that the sum he gave me was the exact figure of the solicitor's demand! I told him that I would take the money to the woman that same day and would leave an envelope with her addressed to him. He wanted to let the gift be anonymous but I insisted otherwise. I always felt that this incident was an example of the truth that if we have done all we can in His guidance and power and still feel our duty has not been completed, we can rely on His providential completion.

I do not think there is any greater joy on earth that that of the calling of a preacher of the Gospel, be he ministerial or lay. I have found the study of preaching to be one of the most fascinating subjects and after nearly sixty years of its practice I am still a learner. From the very beginning, I have always sought to become a better craftsman in the art of preaching. In the very early years, I had the temerity to write to three of the greatest preachers of the day, each of whom I had heard preach. They were J. H. Jowett, who was then described as 'The Prince of Preachers'; John H. Hutton, described by the American Preacher, Dr. Fort Newton, one-time minister of the City Temple, London, in these words: 'In my humble judgment he is the greatest preacher in Britain'; and W. E. Orchard, whose preaching at King's Weigh House Church, London, most certainly justified his position as one of London's greatest preachers. It amazed and humbled me that such great and busy men should take the trouble they did to help an unknown youth as is evidenced by the letters retained in my personal file.

* * *

'All members of the Methodist Church shall have their names entered on a Class Book, shall be placed under the pastoral care of a Class Leader and shall receive a ticket of membership.' This is one of the Church's time-honoured rules. In my early teens I became a member of a Methodist Class which was conducted on what is now described as old-fashioned lines, every member being called upon by name each week to make his or her personal contribution to the testimonies and experiences shared. I became a leader of a class in my late teens and have had the privilege for 55 years – without doubt one of the most important formative influences in my life.

My present class began when six young men of my own church at Dilston Road, Newcastle upon Tyne, asked if I could help them to grow in knowledge and experience of the Christian life. I did not then realize quite how wonderful was the opportunity given to me of God by this invitation. For me it would mean devoting a night every week and for them the same discipline. We ultimately agreed to meet on a Tuesday night in my own home at 7.30 p.m. It was December 1932. When we reached the following July, I asked whether, like most church meetings, we should cease to meet in the holiday months, but they were unanimously in favour of continuing. The result is that to date we have not missed holding the meeting every Tuesday evening for over 40 years. I cannot conceive the extent of the blessing I have received from this wonderful fellowship. Throughout the Second World War, with black-out and air raids, the meetings continued without interruption.

The original young men, in many cases, moved to different parts of the country and the world, and the meeting is now, for the most-part, of middle aged and older men. Several became full-time ministers, local preachers, Sunday School teachers and other officers in the Church. More than one member has designated it the 'power house' for effective service and witness in the Church and the world. I still possess my first class book of 1932 for this Fellowship. John Wesley's preferred number for such a meeting was twelve, as for the first disciples of Jesus. The larger the number, the more difficult is the intimate sharing and participation of each member.

We seek to avoid becoming too formal or lacking in flexibility as it would be easy to get into a rut, and a rut can become a grave. Usually there are two or three hymns, a Bible reading and shared commentary on a passage relevant to the subject to be discussed later. An all-important feature, which has received unanimous appreciation from all who have met with us over the years, is what we call the Prayer Fellowship. People and causes are described by members desiring prayer for them. There is never a shortage of requests and a book could be written of the wonderful answers received.

I have a list of all the subjects discussed over these many years (about 2000), and quote here a few more recent subjects chosen:

'What are the chief temptations of a Christian?'

'I always make a rule of . . . what is one of your rules of life?'

'What is the future of our denominations? Can we justify their continuance to the rising generation?'

"What did Jesus Himself believe? Do you really believe the same?'

'In what ways can we show that the Gospel is relevant to this age?'

'What are the differences between a real Christian and a non-Christian?'

'A place that is especially dear to you – and why?'

'The problem of suffering.'

'What do you regard as answers to prayer?'

'How would you seek to commend Christ to:

(a) A Schoolboy;   (b) A University Student;
(c) A Factory Worker; (d) Someone bereaved,
    none of whom has a personal experience of Christ?'

'What are the main evils in the world today? What are we as individuals doing about them?'

'Am I able to speak naturally of my faith in God in daily conversation? If not, why not?'

'Do you think the ordinary services in your church could be made more helpful, and if so, how?'

'In simple language, what has Christ done for you?'

The Press and broadcasting by sound or television suggest subjects. As an example, I recall the B.B.C. programme 'First Impressions' and the panel which had to decide who the person hidden from their sight was by the answers they gave – via the voice of the compère – to their questions. I once adopted and adapted it for my Fellowship, putting the following questions, which members were asked to answer:

1. Church-going is to me . . . .
2. So far as Sunday is concerned, I . . .
3. Total abstinence is to me . . .
4. Can you conceive of a condition in your life in which it would be true to say 'I've lost everything'?
5. When I am depressed, I . . .
6. It's my belief that . . .
7. If I hear of someone who has spoken critically behind my back, I . . .
8. What are the sins which delay the coming of a better world?
9. I wish I could . . .
10. My greatest ambition is . . . .

(Quoted in *Through the Year with William Barclay*, ed. D. Duncan)

Regularly we devote an evening to personal testimony to God's blessings in home, holidays, work, leisure, personal encounters, experiences and friends.

The older form of Methodist Class Meeting has suffered a decline, partly because of newer forms of Church Fellowship, such as Wesley Guild, Women's Fellowship Meetings, and Young Wives' Clubs, and the multiplicity of other good meetings, but mainly because it became stale in testimony and lost much of the zeal to bring others to know Christ and to enjoy a living fellowship in Him. I was once asked this question.

'How do you maintain a class meeting for years?' This was the answer I gave.

'*I* don't – but if it is a real fellowship, created in Christ by the Holy Spirit, that same creative Spirit will maintain, sustain and provide never-failing freshness in vision and service.'

I have lived to see the Methodist Class Meeting, or weeknight group meeting for prayer, Bible study and discussion of the outreach and application of our faith, become more and more appreciated by the Church of England and other Churches.

As recently as my grandmother's time, the Methodist tradition of 'Cottage Meetings' was still in evidence and now today we are witnessing a revival of interest in what are called 'House Groups'. Bishop Wickham regards the Methodist Class Meeting as possessing one of the finest missionary possibilities for the present-day Church and as a valuable asset for the Church which is to be. The Oxford Group, as it was originally called, now M.R.A.; the Trade Union Movement; the Labour party and the Communist movement; all copied the cell idea or group method, owing not a little to the pioneer work of the small group meetings of the early Methodist Class Leaders.

House groups of this kind in which Christians can 'grow in grace, and in the knowledge of our Lord and Saviour Christ' as Peter exhorted early Christians, are increasing wherever the Church is alive, whether it be in village or city or University and College Christian Societies. My very dear friend, the Rev. 'Bill' Gowland who has accomplished such fine pioneer industrial chaplaincy work as Principal of Luton Industrial Mission, has always believed that the next step for a Christian convert is to become a member of such a group.

Many years ago, we printed a small folded card of invitation to the Fellowship to be used to invite others to join us. One page headed 'WHAT WE SEEK' had three subdivisions:

1. A deeper experience of the friendship of Christ. 2. A richer experience of friendship with each other and with all Christians, whatever their denomination or organization.

3. To make known the friendship of Christ to those who do not enjoy a personal experience of His presence in their lives. A final page was headed, 'WHAT WE DESIRE'; and made these points: 1. A finer Christian life, 2. A united Church, and 3. A better world.

To learn to study the Bible and pray together, to share with each other what God has revealed of His truth in our own experience, to help each other in temptation, trial, failure and success, to encourage each other in winning others to faith and fellowship in Christ – these are some of the potentialities which, continually expressed in personal witness in the world, carry immeasurable possibilities. Also, at both the Men's and Women's Fellowships we have a box on the table into which members place gifts as they feel guided by God. The list of people and causes to which these have been distributed over the years is but one example of our God-directed outreach to the needy.

We should pray for hearts like Wesley's which know no boundaries in prayer and service – to use his own description, 'The world is my parish'. But we should recognize, too, that the number of people we can minister to 'in depth' is limited and follow again our Lord's example ('Thine they were, and Thou gavest them to me') by giving concentrated service to those for whom God has given us especial responsibility. It is true that 'the light that shines the farthest shines the brightest nearest home'.

As the outcome of my own experience, I am convinced that a weekly vital fellowship meeting, to translate our thought and aspiration of Sunday worship into Christian daily living, is essential to progress in Christian discipleship and witness. It should be a priority, as it was in the hearts of those young men who first asked me to lead such a fellowship for them.

Camp meetings held on Sundays on various farms in Northumberland provided another glorious opportunity for Christian fellowship and witness. It was truly remarkable how far the country folk would walk to the afternoon and evening meetings – if fine, held outside, otherwise in a barn. Speaking at one of the barn meetings, I remember that when I rose to give the address, a shepherd's dog came forward, stood at my side, facing the audience seated on straw bales, and remained close beside me to the end of my remarks, then walked back to to join the company for the closing hymn. On another such occasion, as I drew near to the end of my address, a hen somewhere concealed in the hay stored just behind me, set up an enormous and continuous cackle having, no doubt, laid an egg – much to the amusement of the girls and boys present.

Missions in what now seems those far-off days in the 30's were often ecumenical. For example, at Bellingham Town Hall and also at Otterburn I had a Church of England vicar, a Presbyterian minister, Baptist and Methodist ministers joining in the team, along with lay witnesses, night by night. I have had the privilege over 58 years of proclaiming the Gospel at the request of Church of England, Presbyterians, Church of Scotland, Baptists, Brethren, Pentecostalists, Congregationalists, Quakers, Independent Missions and, of course, Methodist Churches. In November 1971, I gladly accepted an invitation to address a joint meeting of the University of Durham Roman Catholic and Methodist Student Societies – a privilege I shall never forget. I find that whatever label we may have, as churches or gatherings of the people of God, there is a fundamental unity which John Wesley expressed in these words: 'If thy heart is as my heart, give me your hand'.

The work which reminded me most of my earlier years in Newcastle Methodist Mission was that done by a remarkable Christian of a remarkable Methodist family, the Bowrans. George Bowran had established the Prudhoe Street Mission, which celebrated its Diamond Jubilee in 1970. For over 40 years I have been associated with this splendid work as a Trustee and for a period as Chairman, and remain a member of its Committee. A greatly appreciated feature was the Destitute Men's Refuge, where a meal, a service and a night's shelter were provided for the 'down and outs' (as I heard them described). In many other ways, as for instance the care of the aged, outings for the poor to the seaside and country, meetings for women and children's gatherings, George Bowran, who died in 1946, demonstrated the truth of the whole Gospel for the whole man, caring for the bodies as well as the souls of men and women.

In complete contrast to Prudhoe Street Mission is the setting of a service which I have shared several times over the years. It is held in a field beside a thorn tree under which is a large stone bearing the following inscription:

John Wesley preached here on his 79th birthday, June 17th 1782'.

When the weather is favourable, the people, as on my first visit, sit on the grass and the view south extending for miles over Northumberland acres is one never to be forgotten.

The Wesley Tree Service, as it is called, is held annually on the nearest Sunday to June 17th, and although I have been unable to trace the exact year when this remembrance service began, I know that it has been held for at least 100 years. The tree stands on the Wallington estate (now the largest held by the National Trust) which was formerly owned by Sir Charles Trevelyan. On one occasion he took me into his study and showed me the desk at which Macaulay wrote his essays.

'You said John Wesley was the greatest Englishman who ever lived and one of the greatest men in the world. I'll show you the greatest man.' He took me to a picture on the wall of Lenin autographed, 'With good wishes to Charles.' 'That's the greatest man,' he said.

'Well, I think you'll agree, Sir Charles, that every man is entitled to his opinion and I'll stick to mine,' I replied, and we parted good friends. To his credit let it be said that he never missed a Wesley Tree Service when at home and always insisted that his house party should accompany him.

If I had my life here to live over again, I would desire more than ever to have the privilege of fulfilling the functions of a preacher and leader in the faith and fellowship of the Christian gospel.

*   *   *

From boyhood I have in particular been greatly interested

in what I came to know as personal evangelism. I caught its
purpose and value from my father, the finest exponent of it I
have ever known. As I like to define my terms, for me it
means bringing men and women, one by one, to know Christ
and commit their lives to Him. All my life I have witnessed
this miracle of the changed life through a firsthand personal
experience of a living relationship to Jesus Christ. Several
changed lives in my boyhood days left an indelible impression on my life as I came to know them as friends. As my
life developed they led to what has been a life-long passion
to share what I know of the Gospel which is Christ, with
those who have not yet received a personal experience of His
saving, guiding and transforming friendship.

The most crowded folders in my filing cabinet, labelled
'Changed Lives', contain letters from young and older
people for whom God has enabled me to do just what
Andrew did for his brother Peter when he 'brought him to
Jesus' (John 1:42). In addition, the book I treasure most
next to my Bible, is my 'Prayer Book'. Commenced in 1930,
it contains the names and addresses of all those who, in
church services or elsewhere, have responded to the simple
invitation to accept Christ's offer of conversion or deeper
consecration and who voluntarily desired me to have their
names for prayer. Let it be said to the glory of God alone
that there are now several thousands of such names, but so
indexed that I can find any name, with the place and date,
within a minute or two. To this day, rarely a Sunday passes
without new names being added.

This Prayer Book, which each year has expanded, provides for me a record of spiritual romance. Constantly I
meet people who stop me in the street or elsewhere and say:
'I have one of your cards', referring to the decision card
which I give to all who make this definite commitment.
Thereupon, after a few words of greeting and inquiry, I

promise that when I return home I will turn up the entry in my Prayer Book and that very evening name them in my private devotions. It is beyond my capacity to number how many times after such encounters, I have remembered in prayer, Charles Wesley's thrilling words:

> 'Tis worth living for this
> To administer bliss,
> And salvation in Jesus' Name.

I also made a point of sending on the names and addresses whenever possible to the Minister concerned, with the request that I might return once to meet them and any friends they desired to invite at either a special week-night meeting convened for this purpose or a suitable regular meeting at the church.

Not long after commencing the Prayer Book I made a decision which proved of outstanding importance in my work of personal evangelism. I decided to reserve every Saturday evening from 6.0 p.m. onward for interviews in my study with men and women seeking an answer to moral and spiritual problems. For over thirty years I have been a fisher of men and women for Christ in this way, which often involves more than one such meeting with an individual, for no one would describe fishing as something one can accomplish in a hurry. I thus discovered what a need exists for confession to one who can be trusted and confided in as a friend who just desires to be of help. Three or more a night was usual but on occasions double this number. Obviously as many others can testify (my son, a minister, allots Monday evening at his church for the same purpose) it means the dedication of time which could be used in other ways, but I cannot possibly tell how much I have received from this work, so exhausting yet exhilarating, arduous yet gloriously rewarding.

One night my wife recalls that I had in the study a Polish Jew, in another room a Roman Catholic, in yet another were three policemen, while she entertained a 'down-and-out' in the kitchen. Under the particular circumstances it would not have been tactful to have had them waiting all together! It is absolutely true to say that I have thus encountered all sorts and conditions of men, from discharged prisoners to University students and professional men and women. To listen, to seek, to understand, to pray with such and above all to enable the Holy Spirit to do His own work in both revealing the need and meeting it in Jesus Christ, was and is my constant aim.

I have chosen one or two examples of such changed lives. If I had known only one of these lives, I would never have doubted the uniqueness of the power of God in Jesus Christ to remake human life, for 'If any one is in Christ, he is a new creation' – I know it because I've seen it. Did not that great Christian, Archbishop Temple, in commenting on the words I have already quoted, 'and he brought him to Jesus', write that this was 'the greatest service one man can do another'?

My first story might be entitled 'A Twentieth Century Prodigal Son'. It is about Stanley, a man who after demobilization following the 1914–18 war came back to share with his brother a prosperous wholesale and retail family business, built up by the arduous labours of his father and mother. At first all went well. Then it was discovered that Stanley's brother was surreptitiously breaking the agreement and, after a tremendous row, the rift between the brothers was complete and was to last over most of thirty years. Stanley continued to develop his part of the business by opening other shops and by the late twenties had a personal income of £4,000 a year – a considerable sum in those days – and about £40,000 capital. He was generous and kind-hearted and, amongst his private charities, gave liberally to the Salvation Army for whom he had a great admiration.*

Stanley was brought up in a Christian home and with his parents belonged to an Independent Baptist Church in South Shields, where in time he began to preach and was in demand as a preacher for other churches. Then suddenly all was changed. He quarrelled with a member of the church and left, gave up preaching and attending worship and 'gave up God', as his son puts it. He lost interest in his business, got in with a 'fast set' and entered into a 'life of riotous living' including bottle parties, theatres, dances and champagne. He had a private box at the Theatre Royal, Newcastle upon Tyne, and times out of number had to be driven home in his own car from well-known restaurants in Newcastle, having been found under the table, hopelessly incapable. His health naturally suffered from his wild, undisciplined life, especially as he had come back from the war with the after-effects of gas attacks which remained a physical handicap.

One Wedneseday, John (the son) called at his father's office to lunch with him. As he entered the main shop he heard a crash and met his Uncle John racing downstairs from his father's first floor office.

'My God – he's taken poison – he's taken poison!'

The fact was that he realized that through neglect of his business, advantage had been taken of his carelessness, his own cost of living had resulted in his becoming penniless in three years, and the car, the servants, the house and all else would have to go. Realizing what it would mean to his wife and family, he had, in a fit of despair, grabbed a full bottle of Lysol, smashed the top off and tossed the contents down his throat. He was taken unconscious by ambulance to the hospital. To everybody's surprise, because of immediate, efficient treatment, Stanley slowly recovered. As he returned

* I rely for many of the details which follow on his son's account.

to consciousness a day or two later he became aware of drops of water on his face. A dear old Salvation Army officer, a friend of many years, was sitting at his bedside and it was his tears that were dropping on the cheek of the still figure in bed. Stanley's eyes flickered, then opened. In a feeble voice he said: 'I've made a bloody mess of this as I have of everything else', and then lapsed into unconsciousness again.

In time he got better and was discharged from the hospital. He was now turned out of the business and his father and mother refused to be reconciled to him. His family continued to attend the Baptist Church known as Bethesda and at the morning service on Sunday, July 28th, 1935, I was announced as the preacher for the evening service. Now let Stanley's son John tell the sequel:

'It seemed to me that father might be persuaded to go with my brother and me to the evening service. I said to him: "We were wondering whether you would care to come down to Bethesda tonight, Dad – there's a fellow from King's College preaching and at least you shouldn't be bored." I waited for fireworks – but none came. Very quietly he said: "I'll think about it."

'That evening will live forever in my memory. I can remember little of the sermon, save that it was based on the text: "Ye must be born again." I do recall how at the close the preacher made an appeal, asking for a response. Before the astonished eyes of the congregation there stood three people at the communion rail, a middle aged woman, a chum of mine, now a Baptist Minister – and father. That night after we had finished supper, we knelt together as a family and asked God's blessing on our new beginning. The transformation in father was astounding – he was a new man. Life in the home was different – there was a sunshine that unemployment and financial difficulty could not dim. Home had been hell! – now it was a place where Jesus reigned.'

Soon after his conversion, I was stopped by a stranger in Grainger Street, Newcastle, who told me he had heard of Stanley's decision to give himself to Christ.

'Don't count on it,' he said to me, 'he's sure to let you down. I know him and he'll not stand, so don't be disappointed.'

What the stranger did not realize was that 'He is able also to save them to the uttermost that come unto God by Him' (Hebrews 7: 25). From that Sunday evening in 1935 Stanley lived a blameless Christian life for nearly 20 years until the moment when he was called to the higher service and "promoted to Glory" (as his Salvation Army friends would affirm).

The revolutionary change in his father's life was a constant challenge to his son John. He began to suspect, and then became convinced, that here was something that he – with all his chapel-going – lacked. One Saturday in September, there was an outing of our Men's Fellowship to a country chapel, where they gathered in the evening for an epilogue. There he came to realize that the thing that was spoiling his life was his intense bitterness towards his father.

Years earlier, a man had called to see his father, who was an old school friend, to ask his help for his son who had the opportunity to go to a University to take a degree, but they could not afford the expense. After making sure of the boy's ability and the father's limited resources, Stanley wrote out a cheque for £1,000.

Stanley's own son had hoped to become a brain-surgeon and now, because of the change in the family fortunes, a career in medicine was impossible. He had never forgotten the £1,000 his father had given to his school chum for his son's career. He could never forgive him for having helped others at the expense of his own. His bitterness was turning his whole life sour.

Again he can remember little of what transpired that September evening, but this he does recall, that Christ entered his life and took possession, and heartache and despair, hatred and disappointment were gone forever. He became a new man – the man God had always intended he should be. He is now a Presbyterian elder.

I first met Redge Cameron in the home of Fred Johnson, a dear friend of mine, then living at Whitley Bay, who had a small group which met weekly in his home for conversation and coffee. I sensed a rather stubborn opposition to acceptance of the faith which I longed that he should come to know. Some months later I was due to preach at Whitley Bay. Redge decided to come to the service. At the end of it he made his way to me.

'When can I see you today?'

'I'm going for lunch to my friend's home,' I replied. 'Can you come round to see me there at 2 o'clock?'

That afternoon my friend and I wrestled with the devil for a man's soul. At last, feeling defeated, I said:

'You say you don't believe what I say, but I think deep down you would like to be able to believe it'. There was a brief silence; then he spoke.

'What you say is right. I've preached it!'

'Let's all kneel and pray,' I said. In the middle of my prayer, he jumped up.

'Let me out of here!' he shouted, and he almost flung himself out, banging the front door behind him. I did not conceal my apprehension.

'He's either going to take his life or find it.'

The next morning, as I came down for breakfast, the phone rang. It was my friend speaking.

'I've just opened a letter by this morning's post from Redge. He has found new life and surrendered everything to Christ.'

That was the beginning, but how wonderful the sequel! Here is a part of it which I personally witnessed.

When I had met Redge that Sunday afternoon, I only knew that he was on the dole and was dressed, as I was, as a layman. It was his remark, 'I've preached it,' which intrigued me. I came to know, through his personal witness, and in conversation, what had preceded that never-to-be-forgotten Sunday afternoon.

Recently he had been a minister at the Baptist Church at Consett, Co. Durham. One night, presiding at a deacons' meeting there, he had lost his temper, flung the minute book on the floor, walked out of the church in every sense, vowing he would never return and taking his wife and family out with him – hence the dole for which he joined the queue regularly. No words can adequately describe the heroic love and loyalty of his wonderful wife in the poverty they were forced then to experience. I once asked him how he ever came to adopt such a drastic and tragic action. He replied: 'For months spiritual dry rot had set in and I found a canker in my soul which destroyed my faith.'

The first night he attended my Fellowship Group, my own brother, Arthur, who was a faithful member of the Group, as we walked home, said: 'Who was that new man there tonight? I've seen him before somewhere.' Before we reached home my brother said:

'I've got it! One night when I was in Sunderland I went to the Town Hall to a debate on Total Abstinence. That man spoke on behalf of the brewers' campaign and seemed to get the better of his ministerial opponent. He made such an able speech and replies to questions.'

Then came a day when I was conducting a mission at Consett at our Methodist Church, and I said to Redge: 'I've prayed much about this request, and I want you to do the same. Will you come and give your personal testimony after my address?' Some days later he said: 'You don't realize how much you are asking me, but I feel that it is God's call and I'll come.' That night, in response to my appeal, a number of men and women making their decision for Christ joined me at the Communion Rail. I saw Redge speaking to an older man and I heard each say, 'It was my fault'. Then Redge whispered to me. 'This was my elder in the church here' and introduced me to him. Through tears the latter said: 'My daughter is kneeling at the Communion Rail and I must be reconciled with my old pastor.' So they both retired to the privacy of the vestry and God did the rest, as they knelt before Him in penitence and faith.

With regular attendance at my Men's Tuesday Fellowship, Redge began to find increasing opportunities for witness in team work and in occasional preaching services. I prayed continuously that the way would open for him to get back on to the Roll of the Baptist Ministry, from which his name had been struck off. I told Redge of my prayer, but he held out no hope, nor did some eminent Baptist ministers and laymen in whom I also confided.

Some months later, I was asked to preach at a nearby Presbyterian Church, but was already booked elsewhere. So, when asked if I could suggest anyone else, at short notice I undertook to see if my friend Redge Cameron could go. This he did and proved very acceptable and received an invitation to return.

The next move in God's wonderful plan was a phone call from the Presbyterian minister responsible to the Presbytery for this particular church, asking if I knew any suitable person who, for a month or two, could do visitation in the area and take services in order to try to build up the cause there. I suggested my friend again for a trial period. The result was an invitation to a full-time pastorate, which after the preliminary period, was confirmed and continued for two years where he and his wife exercised a wonderful ministry.

I then heard that Wyclif Baptist Church, quite near to my home, was seeking a new pastor. Immediately I informed Redge, but he felt it was no use applying, as he was still regarded by some Baptists as under a cloud. Three applications from others were made, who for one reason or another in the end withdrew, and then my friend yielded to my persuasion, after prayer in which we both received the assurance that it was God's call. His application was accepted, and his pastorate at Wyclif Baptist Church over a period of seven years convinced everyone that it was indeed the call of God. After that, he was called to the pastorate of Stanningley Baptist Church in the West Riding of Yorkshire. Here he ministered with the same utter dedication and convincing witness to the indwelling Holy Spirit and the power of the Gospel of Christ, so ably helped by his wonderful Christian wife, Lilla. A failure in health after four years in this pastorate led to his retirement to live at Morpeth, Northumberland, and a disease which wasted his body but could not impair his radiant and virile faith culminated in his passing to the higher service in 1952 at the age of 68 years. I was privileged to give the address at the funeral service at Wyclif to a crowded church, which included several members who came from Stanningley, each to pay their last respects to a beloved and truly faithful pastor and friend.

Whenever I think of my dear friend and the change from standing in the queue for dole to a pulpit, resulting in years of blessed ministry to the salvation and eternal enrichment of many souls, I am reminded of William Cowper's well known hymn: 'God moves in a mysterious way His wonders to perform' – *but He moves*. You can imagine, therefore, with what joy I read the following telegram from Redge at

Bloomsbury Baptist Church, London, where he was attending the Baptist Annual Congress meetings: 'Back in the lists (of Accredited Baptist ministers) Alleluia, Redge.' For 'the years that the locusts had eaten' God gave him 13 years in the full-time, active ministry.

The story of Jack Harrison, the miner who became one of my dearest friends, began on the 'wonderful Sunday evening' described by Dr. Sangster in his *Westminster Sermons (Vol. 1)*, an occasion when I was the preacher:

'I remember a day I once spent in County Durham with a friend of mine – a coal miner. He is a man in middle life now. Before his conversion, he was a drunken sot. He was a cheat as well. Playing once in a dominoes competition, he covered a dot with a bit of chewing gum and cleared the "kitty" of £29. He had a good mother and a good wife, and he came near to breaking the hearts of both of them. One day his mother said to his wife: "Leave him, Nellie. Leave him! He'll drag you to hell."

'But Nellie didn't leave him, nor ceased to pray, and one wonderful Sunday evening she had the answer to her prayers. Spent up and miserably sober, he yielded to her pleading and went with her to evening worship where a friend of mine was preaching his characteristically powerful evangelical word. When at the end of the sermon, my friend made an appeal, Jack stumbled forward and asked God to forgive him.

'What an hour! I think he only ever glanced back once . . . and it was but a glance. He was transformed in the astonished gaze of all the neighbourhood. In the passing of only a few years, the Holy Spirit wiped from his face all the marks of dissipation and made him radiant with an unearthly light.

'When I first knew him, I had been ordained twice as long as he had been converted, and there are some things I can do, I suppose, that he can't do. But oh! there are many important things that *he* can do which I can't do. It is wonderful to hear him talk to men who have missed their way; such love, such incisiveness, such skill with sinners ... I know he has travelled the road of Christian discipleship faster than I have done.'

From *Bristol Fashion* by the late Hugh Redwood – one time Religious Editor of the *News Chronicle* and author of *God in the Slums* and several other books, writes of the same miner:

'Facing me for my inspiration, as I sat at my desk in the office, is a photograph taken in the house of a miner in Durham, where a Fellowship of some fifty members, many of them converted there, meet every Sunday night in order to gather strength for the coming week's witness. The photograph shows that almost all belong to just that class of young people with whom the Church is so greatly pre-occupied. They have sent a missionary of their own to Africa, but they are all missionaries where they live and work. They win their parents, their work-mates, the people they contact over the counter. Three of them are nurses in a hospital fifteen miles away, but they cycle that distance, when duty permits, to take their part in the fellowship meetings, and afterwards cycle back again. Thirty miles at the end of the day to meet with God in a miner's dwelling. Tell that to the empty down-town churches. Last year a team of these same young people spent several days in a Yorkshire town speaking for Christ in the market place. Communists wanted to know who paid them, and learned that each of them put down £5 as his or her share of the expenses. Tell that to defaulting witnesses, and to those, if any, who still believe that religion, in a world like ours, is too sacred a thing to be aired in public.'

No man ever enjoyed more loving, loyal and steadfast

friends than I possess in Jimmy and Sarah Gilliland. They live in an unpretentious house in a row at Chopwell (once famed in the General Strike for a rumoured establishment of a Soviet community). Jimmy was a bus conductor, now retired, who, before his conversion, made his home a hell, and was on the point of leaving his wife, having more than once told her to quit. He looks back with remorse on those days when through selfishness and meanness and mental cruelty he hardly conversed with her. Then on January 23rd 1938 he was converted and his home has become a foretaste of heaven, as I and all who have ever been within its walls can fully confirm. Jimmy found increasing spiritual life after his conversion – the life 'more abundant' as Christ described it – in my Tuesday Fellowship for many years, and now attends a Fellowship meeting at his own church on the same evening.

I remember one Sunday morning, soon after his conversion, he accompanied me in my car to a preaching engagement along the Tyne Valley. It was a beautiful morning, and to Jimmy the lovely countryside, the sun shining through the trees, the autumn tints and the sights to which he drew my attention inspired him with wonder and joy. It was as though he had been blind and had just recovered his sight, and in a perfectly natural way he went into rhapsodies.

I never forget how he remarked: 'You know, I never knew what a beautiful world it was until Christ came into my heart.'

'It is never too late to mend.' The words 'too late' remind me of two girls in their late teens who attended an evening service I conducted in 1951. It was Youth Sunday, and in the words of John Wesley, at the close of the service 'I offered them Christ.' I then invited any who had heard His call or desired to talk over with me how to become a Christian to meet me in the minister's vestry after the service. To my great joy five young men and four young women came to the vestry, all of whom made a personal commitment to Christ. All this took considerable time and when they had gone, I followed the steward to the side door of the church, which he locked and then we shook hands and said: 'Good-night'. Suddenly round the corner from the front of the church two girls rushed up and halted suddenly, panting for breath.

'Is it too late?'

'If you mean to give yourself to Christ, no,' I replied.

They had left the service and started to go on their favourite walk to the end of Tynemouth Pier. For a long time they walked in silence and then one said: 'I ought to have stayed behind to see the preacher', to which her friend said: 'Do you mean that? Because I feel the same'. So they ran and walked with only seconds to spare. When I read the story of the young man who ran to Jesus to ask for the secret of eternal life (see Mark 10: 17) I always think of the two girls who ran that night to the Saviour.

Both have remained loyal to their vows. One of them, whose Christian name is Jean, and is now Mrs. Hickman, has a family of three lively girls. She called to see me in November 1970. I had not seen her for about fifteen years, for she and her husband spent their days making guests comfortable and happy at the Royal Victoria Hotel, Nassau, in the Bahamas.

All through my life I have seen these wonders of His grace; bad men made good and good men made so much better, and all – whether man or woman, young or older – being enabled to receive the more abundant life Christ came, as He declared, to make possible. In recent days I rejoice to hear of changed lives like those of Cliff Richard, the actor James Fox, and others. That it is only when we are at our best for God that we can be at our best for His children, I regard as one of the most important discoveries I ever made.

There is some confusion in these days as to what constitutes a Christian. In the recent, much discussed book *Secular Evangelism* written by Fred Brown, the author argues that there are more Christians outside the Church than in it. I recognize there are many good people who are outside the Church. That they are outside is often symptomatic of either a loss of faith in Christ or never having possessed this personal relationship with Him. Some are living on the spiritual capital bequeathed to them through Christian forbears, but in any case all goodness is inspired by the Holy Spirit *whether He is acknowledged or not.* Nevertheless, I believe a Christian is one who has committed himself or herself to Christ and seeks to follow Him faithfully.

My son, Baptist pastor at Guildford, had the opportunity at one of his services of putting questions to Cliff Richard.

'What had you to give up when you became a Christian, Cliff?' was the first question. Cliff gave the perfect answer in one word:

'Myself'.

'If any man will come after me, let him deny himself . . .' – in other words put himself for ever second. Or should I not say third? – recalling an address I heard many years ago on joy – Jesus first, Others second, and Yourself last of all.

It is good to win a man or woman in middle life or old age for Christ but what wonderful possibilities lie in the decision of youth. That is why I have always sought to win the young people to His service which is perfect freedom; and looking at an excellent photograph of Jean Hickman and her husband and three little girls which she gave to us on her recent visit, how thankful I was that their daughters have been granted the priceless blessing of a Christian home.

6

Lover of Home

'O happy home, where two in heart united
In holy faith and blessed hope are one'.

In September 1927, I married Jean Sinclair, daughter of the
late Mr. John Sinclair of Newcastle and Heathcote, Allen-
dale, and thus began a partnership which resulted in a happiness no words can possibly describe and without which –
whatever other success I might have achieved – I cannot
conceive how impoverished my life and experience would
have been.* All through the years of a blissfully happy married life we have shared the many-coloured experiences of
life, finding increasingly our oneness in our love for God and
His love for us. Our sorrows and sufferings as well as joys and
happiness have all contributed to this oneness. We have
shared everything, including one banking account!

We have been blessed with three children, two girls and a
boy, all three ultimately making their new homes in Manses,
and giving us our nine grandchildren. Every Sunday after
lunch my wife and I continued the practice commenced
when we began our married life of having family prayer,
taking turns to lead on alternate weeks. It is well known,
therefore, not only to friends but to our children and grandchildren that they are faithfully remembered, not only in
our daily private devotions, but in this special additional
way on Sundays. I often say that one of the greatest blessings

*In an earlier book, *Personal Evangelism*, which I dedicated to her, I
wrote: 'I have endeavoured many times to find words with which to ex-
tend this dedication, but have failed – the debt I owe to her is not
only incalculable but beyond words'.

God has bestowed upon us is that, whilst concerned from time to time about our children's physical troubles, we have never had a single worry in all the years concerning their moral and spiritual welfare. The joy we have in those whom God has given to us is another experience which cannot be communicated in words.

The greatest sorrow of our married life was the passing of our younger daughter, Ruth, at the early age of thirty-two years, after twelve years of happy married life, leaving a husband and two children. She was stricken with an incurable disease at 30 years of age. God brought us through a two-year trial of faith and the last few months of agonizing vicarious suffering. One of our dearest friends, Mrs. W. E. Sangster, with whom we stayed to be near enough to Westminster Hospital, London, for our daily visits to our daughter, right to the last, was used of God, as were so many other friends, to mediate His comfort to us. She said to us, arising out of her own experience: 'Time lessens the pain but the ache will remain'. How right she was, for only that blessed re-union which is the Christian hope will banish that ache, though we do not doubt that she is alive for evermore, and because of that is still one of us and one with us. The words given to me in the hour when I needed it most were those God inspired William Cowper to write in his hymn: 'God is His own interpreter and He will make it plain'.

We built our house in 1927, the year of our marriage, and we moved in during a snowstorm in December. We love our house, made and kept beautiful as a home by the care and constant improvements made by my wife. Of course, the things which transform a house into a real home are beyond value and could not be listed in the insurance booklet. I remember when Dr. and Mrs. W. E. Sangster, then living on Wandsworth Common, had their house burgled, I wrote to sympathize with them – with some understanding as thieves had broken into Overdale twice – he replied, mentioning some of the things which had been stolen, but concluding with these words: 'But you will know they couldn't rob us of the things we treasure most.'

So many of the material things which we possess are dear to us because of what they recall to us and this is especially true of pictures, though also of other things.

We have no really valuable works of art on the walls of our home, but I love what pictures we have, for each one tells a story. Facing me, as I sit at breakfast each morning, is one of my favourite pictures.

I had long wanted a picture of Durham, for whilst I am Emeritus Professor of both Newcastle and Durham Universities, it was Durham that conferred my degrees and it was a Durham County Scholarship which made possible the beginning of my academic career.

At a well-known Newcastle art shop, the salesman set up three pictures – all within the limit of what I felt I could afford – from which to make my choice. I surprised him by the quickness of my decision – so much so that he said: 'I think it is the best of the three, but I am interested to know how you decided so quickly.' This is what I told him.

When I was in my teens and became a committed Christian, I also became a lay preacher, and one of my heroes, as I have already testified, and will do so again, was John Henry Jowett. In later years, I was privileged to call him my friend and I treasure some of his letters to me. I have all his books on my library shelves.

In one of his smaller books, *The Passion for Souls*, he has an illustration of the words of Micah the prophet: 'The mountain of the house of the Lord shall be established in the top of the mountains and it shall be exalted above the hills.'

'I think of Durham city,' he writes, 'as an emblem of the

prophet's thought. Away in the lower reaches of the city there is the river, on which boats are plying for pleasure and recreation. A little higher up on the slopes are the places of business, the ways and byways of trade. A little higher there is the castle hill on which the turreted tower presents its imposing front; but on a higher summit, commanding all and overlooking all these, rises and towers aloft the majesty of the glorious old cathedral. Let me interpret the emblem. The river is typical of pleasure, the ways of business are representative of money, the castle is the symbol of armaments. In whatever prominence these may be seen, they are all subordinate to the reverence and worship of God.'

On the mantelpiece of my little study are mementoes of visits to other countries we have made in later years. These include a small water pot from Bethlehem, a lamp from the catacombs in Rome, a brass camel from a store in the Street called Straight in Damascus, a model of a Swiss chalet, a 'brass' of a ploughman and his team of horses and small models of a Scotch mountain ewe and lamb which speak of my agricultural interests; also reminders of our visits to America and Norway, as representatives to two World Methodist Conferences, in the form of models of the Statue of Liberty, the 'Queen Mary' on which we travelled and a silver Viking ship.

Above the mantelpiece is a picture of Jesus with His disciples walking through the cornfield, and on one side of this picture is a framed copy of 'Praying Hands' (Dürer's) sent to me by an old lady in Carlisle who faithfully remembers my services in her prayers every Sunday. On the other side is hung an artistic lettered card bearing the words: 'Ask Him'— a wonderful challenging reminder to myself and to others who come to my study with their spiritual and moral problems.

Before leaving the mantelpiece I must mention one last

item. Suspended on the wall at the right end is a section from the branch of a tree, varnished and beautifully printed in black lettering as follows: 'From an Ash at Bay Bridge, Blanchland, in whose shade John Wesley preached.' It was given to me by a colleague on the staff of the School of Agriculture, who did not share my Christian faith, and certainly not my Methodist loyalty, but respected my Christian principles and was always helpful when I sought advice in his subject, which was Agricultural Economics. It happened that one day he visited a Northumbrian farmer who, when they were sitting round his fireside, took a log of wood and having thrown it on the fire, said: 'There goes a bit more of Wesley's Tree.' My friend expressed his curiosity and discovered that a tree on the farm, known for more years than could be remembered as the tree under which Wesley preached, had blown down in a recent gale.

'Can you give me a log?' said my friend.

'I'll give you a sack of them,' was the reply.

'No, one is all I want,' and from that he cut the section and with his gifted craftsmanship this hanging, delightful memento.

What now follows might be described as how I came to know two famous 'R.A.'s' through an unpremeditated aside as I preached one night in our Methodist Church at Chelsea for my son-in-law, then minister of this church. After the service, I shook hands at the entrance with members of the congregation and an attractive, little white-haired old gentleman spoke to me.

'I gathered from a remark you made that you would like to see the grave of Peter Böhler?' – the man, so I believe, who more than any other, was used of God to bring John Wesley the transforming experience out of which came ultimately the Methodist Church.

'I would,' I replied. 'I haven't found a Methodist yet in the thousands of my fellow members who has seen it and I am a great devotee of John Wesley.'

'Here's my card,' he replied. 'Call and see me and I'll take you to it.'

In due course, my son-in-law motored me to his house, where we had coffee, and looking round a very large studio, I realized that Malcolm Osborne must be a very busy artist. We then set off for what to me seemed a wonderful oasis of peace, just off the busy King's Road and after some searching amongst the overgrown grass, found the gravestone to Bishop P. Böhler, the Moravian Christian. Looking round the enclosure – reached through large coachhouse doors, there seemed only the large grass plots and some beautiful trees on the boundary.

Then our host pointed out an old-world cottage dwelling, with what might once have been a stable attached to it.

'A great friend of mine lives there. Have you time to meet her for a few minutes?'

We readily agreed and thus we were introduced to a lady who apparently could not move from her chair, being crippled with arthritis. It did not take me long to realize that she was a rich personality. She told her friend, now our friend too, to show us her studio. This was a spacious interior, probably re-constructed from the stable or coachhouse. My attention was caught first by a fine piece of stone bearing a lovely bronze head and shoulders of the Bishop of Chichester, with an inscription in gold and blue lettering not quite completed. Wandering around, I picked up a yellow clay saucer, bearing an outline of head and shoulders but no lettering, yet somehow I felt I ought to know who was represented. Finally, I picked up a dusty black and white photographic postcard which gave full details of another commemorative plaque.

Returning to the room in which we had left our hostess,

her first question was: 'Well, now, Professor, tell me what has interested you in my studio?' I recounted the three objects I have described. She told me that the memorial to Bishop Bell was to be placed in Chichester Cathedral. Not many weeks later, I saw in *The Times* the report and photograph of the unveiling. Incidentally, she said she had been a little uncertain in getting the frock collar right and a nearby Roman Catholic priest had obliged as a model – shades of ecumenicity!

For the second object – the clay saucer – she asked me if I could produce a shilling or a sixpence.

'I happen to be the designer of the coins for the Royal Mint. Her Majesty the Queen gave me several sittings and they took me in an ambulance car to the Palace.' The final picture was on my sixpence.

'And now, anything else you saw?' she inquired.

'Yes,' I said. 'A photographic card of my wife's favourite singer, Kathleen Ferrier.'

'I'm a bit of a thought reader, Professor,' she said. 'I think you would like that card.'

'I would certainly like to know where I could buy one,' I replied.

'Take that one and give it to your wife with my kind regards,' she insisted. I persuaded her to autograph it, and she wrote on the back: 'Mary Gillick fecit.'

The finished plaque, she informed me, is now to be found in the waiting room of University College Hospital, where the world-famed singer, who (she said) was adored by her nurses, finally succumbed to her tragic illness. It was so commissioned because of the generous Memorial Fund which provided a surplus. Before I said goodbye to the charming lady – a prisoner to her chair, but without a complaint – she told me that a few days after her final visit to the Palace, a car drove up to the large open doors which she could see

through the window where she sat. It was driven by a gentleman who made his way to her door and rang the bell to be
greeted by her call from the chair: 'Come in.' He sat down in
the chair which I was occupying.

'The Queen was anxious to know how you had stood the
strain of the visits to Buckingham Palace.'

After a pleasant talk, the Duke of Edinburgh rose and
entered his car and drove off alone. I don't suppose this
kindly action ever appeared in the Court Circular!

When I returned to Newcastle, I consulted *Who's Who* to
be able to write my letter of thanks and found the names of
my two friends as follows:

> *OSBORNE*, Malcolm, C.B.E. 1948, R.A. 1926; P.R.E.,
> A.R.C.A., President Royal Society of Painter-Etchers and
> Engravers, 1938 . . . Later Professor of Engraving, Royal
> College of Art. A.R.A. 1918.

> *GILLICK*, Mary, O.B.E. 1953, Sculptor . . . m.1905, Ernest
> Gillick, A.R.A. (d.1951). Work includes: Effigy of the Queen
> for the coinage and for official medals . . . to Kathleen Ferrier
> in University College Hospital, London, and other memorials
> in London and in Cambridge. Medals for the Royal Mint, the
> Royal Society, etc.

Subsequently I wrote to Mr. Osborne and as tactfully as I
could explained that I could not afford a large price, but
that I would love some small work of his execution. By
return post came six unframed etchings for me to choose
from. My choice was a delightful one of a spring scene on a
Lake District farm. I informed my friend that I had chosen
it because of our nearness to and love for the Lakes, and in
reply he said that he was delighted with my decision because
he had many happy memories of the district. He and others
of the School of Fine Arts, London, were evacuated there
during the Second World War. So every time I look at his
framed picture hanging on the wall of my dining room, I

recall what I have just described. And it all came out of my desire to see where Peter Böhler was buried!

Perhaps the pictures we have treasured most at Overdale – found in most rooms – are our coloured photographs of our children and grandchildren. One in particular is a favourite, showing, as it does, a group of the whole of our family, standing outside the Dunes Hotel at Seahouses, Northumberland, where for the first time we were able to gather together for a week on the occasion of our 40th Wedding Anniversary.

In addition to the etching in the dining room, there is a coloured picture of Newcastle dated September 22nd, 1761, 'Coronation Day' for King George and Queen Charlotte, showing the Tyne with only one bridge across it, with houses built on the bridge. An added interest to us is that it would be just as it was at the time of John Wesley's visits to Newcastle about this date. There is also a print of John Wesley himself, an engraving from the collection of the famous Thomas Bewick and published in 1781. Another print is of Cockle Park Tower, near Morpeth, with a brief account on the back of the Border raiders, which proves that what has happened in recent years between Israel and Egypt – namely raids and counter-raids – happened in those far-off days in this country. How little the world has changed in some things!

Five small coloured prints have an interesting history. I happened to be in London, and passed a small shop with a few prints in the window. I went in and asked if they had any old prints of Newcastle. I was given a pile of every size and shape to look through and eventually found five delightful little coloured prints of different parts of Newcastle, at a very reasonable price. They are now framed and hang together on the wall of the dining room. That same day in Foyle's I bought a coloured map of the county of Northumberland which now hangs in our hall and is of great interest to visitors as they note how many are the beauty spots and places of interest located in what I consider to be one of the finest counties of England.

An old, irregular, fairly short thorn stick, now polished with age, cut by my grandfather one day in a wood at Salters Gate is the oldest in the rack, for I would be under nine years of age at the time. Then there is a stout walking stick with a small hoe on the end, strong enough to cut a thistle or dock out of the ground, which belonged to my old Professor in Agriculture and was given to me after his death by his widow, Mrs. Gilchrist. I was not only one of his students, but at his invitation became his assistant and friend on completing my College training. There is a fine gold-mounted cane, purchased for me by my wife when we were on honeymoon at Eastbourne. Beside it there is an old-fashioned, horn-handled stick which my grandfather kept for walking to Church on Sunday and other special occasions, with his name on it. When I retired in 1957, I was most touched by the gift of a fine walking stick with a silver band bearing the words: 'From past and present workers to Professor Pawson' reminding me of my long association with the famous agricultural Experimental Station at Cockle Park, where I began in my first job as Record Keeper, and ended as Director. Another unusual stick with a green leather knob was given to me by an African friend, who studied law in Newcastle and London, and is now a Judge in Sierra Leone, and for whom God used me to bring to a personal knowledge of Christ. Beside it is a plain handled stick made by a fine Christian friend in North Devon whose hobby is forestry and who had it made from a tree of his own growing. Finally, a Northumbrian shepherd's stick, with its beautiful horn shaped handle, given to me by my dear Christian farmer friend Tom Hall, was the last addition to my stick stand. Boyhood, manhood, career, marriage, holidays, friends – 'all

the way the Lord thy God hath led thee' for over 75 years –
these are perpetual reminders of them all, with the shepherd's
crook to say to me as I glance at it. 'The Lord is my shepherd,
I shall not lack anything.'

7

Life's Signposts

Who shall say that roads have signposts and that lives have none?
From 'These Three Gentlemen' by A. E. W. Mason.

The title of this chapter is derived from one of my war-time experiences. Some time after the Second World War began, my difficulties in locating farms were increased by the removal of all signposts for the war period. One day I had to visit a hill farm I had never heard of which was in the very heart of the Cheviot country, and I realized I was lost. Soon after, to my relief, a shepherd and his dog appeared on the road. He gave me rather lengthy instructions and then said:

"Look, can I come in the car with you? I will show you exactly where it is.'

Later, I thought of my morning experience with the kindly shepherd as a parable of life – first the knowledge of the guide book, the Bible, then my parents and friends, and then the meeting with Him whom John described as the Way, who came to two who had lost their way in life, though they knew they were on the road to Emmaus. Better than the map or signposts is the One who knows the way and promises to those who trust Him, 'Lo, I am with you always'.

Nevertheless, I am abidingly grateful for a host of men and women who I know have been God's signposts for me, and I select a few, in addition to my parents, whose example pointed me in the right direction, and by whom I have been enriched and enlarged.

One man I greatly admired was Viscount Grey of Fall-

oden, to some of my generation better known as Sir Edward
Grey, the Foreign Minister whose speech in the House of
Commons was decisive in bringing Britain into the First
World War. He was, to me, a signpost of integrity. I write
this tribute to him not many miles from his Northumbrian
home, Falloden, at the holiday fishing village of Seahouses.

One morning in 1970 my wife and I took the road leading
south from Seahouses and in a few miles came to the attractive little village of Embleton.

It was the 'Grey' corner at the back of the church which
was my main objective, for here was the description of the
life's signpost who had influenced me. These are the words
behind the seat he occupied when able to walk over from
Falloden for matins.

> *'In memory of Edward, Viscount Grey of Falloden,*
> *K.G.*
> *Born 25th April 1862. Died at Falloden, 7th September,*
> *1933.*
> *Succeeded his grandfather, Sir George Grey, as third*
> *Baronet, 1882.*
> *M.P. for Berwick-on-Tweed Division, 1885–1916*
> *Secretary of State for Foreign Affairs, 1905–1916*
> *Created Knight of the Garter 1912, and Viscount Grey*
> *of Falloden, 1916*
> *Chancellor of the University of Oxford, 1928.*
> *A statesman – wise, valuable, single-minded –*
> *A friend flawless and faithful.'*

During my forty years in what is now known as the University of Newcastle upon Tyne, I have seen many famous
men and women honoured at Convocations, but high on my
list I place Viscount Grey of Falloden. I consider his biography *Grey of Falloden* one of the finest in the English

language of the present century – a great subject, and a great biographer, Professor G. M. Trevelyan, the former Cambridge Regius Professor of Modern History, and one-time Chancellor of Durham University. What nobility of character and integrity were revealed in Grey, and especially the fortitude with which he bore his experiences of adversity. His beautiful young wife was killed by being thrown out of a trap when the horses shied on one of the roads near Falloden. His two homes, the ancestral Falloden and a modest cottage near Itchen Abbas (to which he would escape from London for short spells of fishing) were both burnt down. The world of peace he endeavoured to maintain was shattered by the First World War, and when he returned to the Foreign Office after his memorable speech in the House of Commons he not only said: 'The lights are going out all over Europe, and will not be lit again in our time', but also crashed his hand on the table and said three times: 'I hate war'.

Most of all, I admired his serenity and complete absence of self-pity in his misfortunes, the greatest of which in his later years being the loss of his sight. It was during that first World War that his sight began to fail, and he was warned by his medical advisors that if he continued with his Foreign Office work he was endangering his sight permanently, but he chose to do what he felt was his duty, bearing in mind the war-time sacrifice of so many, and paid the cost of so doing.

He never complained to his affliction, but actually joked with a friend about being able to read in bed without getting his hands cold – his hands being under the blanket reading Braille, though the capacity to do this became increasingly difficult. Life can either make us bitter or better – only the alteration of one letter, but what a world of difference! Trevelyan writes of him: 'He was a nobler man in the latter part of his life than he had been in the days of his perfect happiness.' A key to his attitude to people and life is afforded by words he expressed to a young man bent on a diplomatic career, who was introduced to him in the hope of a word of counsel from the great statesman. Grey paused for a while and then said: 'Remember that gullibility is always better than suspicion.' Courageous and patient in adversity, cheerful in spirit when health was failing, he was indeed a noble man.

John Henry Jowett, C.H., M.A., D.D., was, next to my father, one of a few examples I took as models of great preaching. He began his ministry at St. James' Congregational Church, Newcastle upon Tyne – a church with a considerable standing and tradition to which he was invited, on completing his student days, to accept the pastorate. Subsequently he became minister at Carr's Lane, Birmingham, then at Fifth Avenue Presbyterian Church, New York, returning for his last pastorate to Westminster Chapel, Buckingham Gate by an invitation which was strongly supported by a personal appeal from the then Prime Minister, Mr. Lloyd George. He became known on both sides of the Atlantic as 'the Prince of Preachers', and as visitors to New York passed his church there, in the city official tours, the guide would indicate the building and describe Jowett as 'the greatest preacher in the English speaking world'. To me he became one of my signposts soon after I began to try to preach. I began to read his published sermons and meditations, and was greatly attracted by his persuasive, lucid style and especially the fine devotional fervour which permeated all his printed prayers and sermons.

One week-end, when as a family we were staying at Wooler, my father took me on Saturday to Edinburgh and, walking up the numerous steps which led from the Waverley Station to Princes Street, he paused near the top (perhaps to get a breather).

'And now I'll tell you why I've brought you to Edinburgh. I've brought you to hear your hero, who is preaching here tomorrow.'

Princes Street was crowded that Saturday afternoon as we walked to our hotel. All I had ever seen was a head and shoulder photograph of the great Dr. Jowett. He never wore the usual ministerial collar. Suddenly, about half way along the famous street, I gripped my father's arm.

'Dr. Jowett, Father! I've seen him.'

'Where? and how do you know?' asked my father.

I really did not know, I just felt that the tall gentleman in a grey suit looking like a solicitor or Harley Street specialist (of those days) walking in a quiet, dignified manner, was my hero. In a few moments my father stopped in front of the gentleman I pointed out.

'Dr. Jowett?'

'That is my name,' he quietly replied.

'May I introduce my son?' I had a thousand things I wanted to say to him and could not get one out. Then at last I gasped:

'We've come to hear you preach, Dr. Jowett.'

'I understand,' he said, 'that tomorrow, owing to re-decoration of the St. George's West Church, they are joining the two congregations at St. George's Parish Church It's just possible it may be a little crowded.'

This was said by the minister who never preached without queues forming outside the church hours before the doors were opened! Taking out his notecase he abstracted a card, gave it to me, took my hand once more and said:

'If you find it difficult, give this to one of the vergers and say *you are a friend of mine*' (my italics). I slept with the card under my pillow.

Arriving a long time before the service, there were long queues at every door.

'There,' I said, in keen disappointment, 'if only we had come sooner as I wanted to, and now we'll never get in.'

As we gradually neared the door of our queue, there was an ominous slowing down. Then my father said: 'Where's that card?' which I was clutching in my hand, and going to a verger said: 'It's not for myself, but if you can possibly squeeze my boy in, I'll be so grateful'. And without, in the end, any jumping of the queue he managed to get us both seats in the completely packed church. That was September 1st, 1918, and I remember as though it were yesterday the silvery voice of the great preacher and his sermons. In the morning he preached from Isaiah 61: 1, and in the evening (for which service we made sure of arriving in good time!) from Matthew 11: 28, and I can still recall some of the points and illustrations he used.

Beneath the pulpit of St. James Congregational Church, Newcastle, where he commenced his great ministry, are his own words in gold lettering: 'I have had but one passion and I have lived for it – the absorbingly arduous yet glorious work of proclaiming the grace and love of our Lord Jesus Christ'. From his student days at Edinburgh University, Jowett's over-mastering ambition was to preach.

During a Methodist Conference in Birmingham, I was asked to 'fill in' at an overflow meeting in Carr's Lane Congregational Church. My two favourite speakers, Drs. Weatherhead and Sangster, were to come over when they had spoken to a main meeting in the Town Hall. Shown into an ante-room at Carr's Lane I met several of the deacons, and asked one if there was a picture of Dr. Jowett anywhere. He took me into what I judged to be the Minister's private vestry and pointed to it on the wall. I forget most of what I said in the address that followed. I do remember that in introducing myself I told the story of my first meeting with Jowett and told my audience that it is one thing to have a picture but how much more real and wonderful to hear him speak to you personally and say 'You're a friend of mine'. It was the same in our relationship to Christ – all of us, no doubt, had a picture from childhood given in home or Sunday School from friends and loved ones but it makes all the difference when He steps out of the frame and is welcomed into our hearts in what my friend Leslie Weatherhead described in the title of his first book (to me perhaps his best one) *The Transforming Friendship*.

When in New York in 1956, I visited Fifth Avenue Presbyterian Church and found my way into the church hall where I knew from his biography, written by Arthur Porrit, that Jowett held his mid-week service, and as I wandered about I saw a lady who obviously was wondering who I was and what I wanted. I told her of my admiration and affection for Dr. Jowett, whereupon she invited me into the minister's vestry to see his picture on the wall and said: 'The room is very much like it was in his time here.' I thanked her for her memories of his ministry and later offered a silent prayer of thanksgiving for the life and work of this great preacher of the Gospel in that great church.

In his few years in London he joined with the Archbishop of York in a National Campaign for Peace, visiting various cities as joint speakers, but his failing physical resources and subsequent illness made it impossible for him to preach at Westminster Chapel on the Sunday set apart for the culmination of the Peace Campaign – a campaign for which he had been largely responsible. I received wonderful letters from him confirming the glorious truth of his own personal experience of trust in God whatever betide. He was about the same age (60 years) as that of my dearest friend, the Rev. Dr. W. E. Sangster, when God called him to the higher service. Jowett influenced me in many ways, especially in the tender, wooing note in his appeal for commitment to God. In those early days of attempting to preach I was too inclined to the strident, challenging, critical, aggressive approach, and I came to realize how much more effective is an all-embracing love for Christ and my fellow men, which characterized my great hero.

I was present in the historic service at evensong on Tuesday, February 15th, 1924, in Durham Cathedral when, at the invitation of Bishop Welldon, then Dean of the Cathedral, Jowett was the preacher. As soon as the preacher mounted the pulpit the then Vicar of Wheatley Hill made a most unseemly and irreverent protest and walked down the aisle in a threatening manner, calling out in a loud voice his objection to Jowett's presence. For a few minutes there were signs of uproar from the vast congregation, and then, near where I was seated, a few miners struck up the hymn 'When I survey the wondrous Cross', which was quickly taken up by the congregation. Jowett, I noticed, went very white, but stood still until the hymn concluded and then, with unruffled serenity, gave out his text and proceeded to preach a great sermon on 'Supplementing the sufferings of Christ'. I am grateful for this opportunity to pay my humble tribute to a signpost I ever remember in gratitude to God.

The Rev. Samuel Chadwick was a father in God to me and, with my father first, shared second place with Dr. Jowett in my trio of hero worship in those early days. He was then Principal of Cliff College, Calver near Sheffield, when I was a Grammar School boy at Bakewell. He had no children of his own, but in his love, friendship, wise counsel and encouragement I felt I was an adopted son. When I think of some of these signposts, who consciously and unconsciously were a source of spiritual direction to me, I sometimes attach to their memory a text from the Scriptures. For Chadwick, I think the most apt words I could apply are those of St. Paul to Timothy, his son in the Gospel – 'Study to show thyself approved unto God, a workman that needeth not to be ashamed, rightly dividing the word of truth' (11 Timothy 2: 15).

Unlike Jowett, he never had the benefit of a University education; indeed he was self-taught, and from the age of eight from 8 o'clock in the morning he was *at work* in a cotton mill. He was converted through a Sunday School Anniversary when he was ten, influenced by a story told by the preacher about Newton, who had said if he were a shoeblack he would be the best shiner of boots in the village. When the preacher talked about shining boots he sat up. Here is how Chadwick himself described the most momentous happening in his life.

'I hated to clean boots, especially father's Wellingtons. The Anniversay was a wet day, boot cleaning next morning was at its worst. I began with the Wellingtons, on the principle that the irksome part of a task is best tackled at once. I got through and put them down with a sense of relief. Then as I looked at them, the preacher's words about shining boots as if Jesus Christ was going to wear them challenged me ... I wondered if those Wellingtons would look well on the feet of Jesus Christ. For answer, I took up the boots and began again. It was a simple thing to do, but I believe, in the light of after years, that it was the most important thing I ever did in my life. It was the adoption of a fixed principle from which I have never gone back. I got into the habit of doing the simplest duties as unto, and for, Jesus Christ.'

When 16 years old, this mill boy began to preach, and in due course entered the Methodist ministry. He became first Tutor and later Principal of the College whose influence has spread throughout the world and still continues, and is now no longer limited to male students. Through the teaching and training of evangelists – many having become full-time ministers – the College has met the need especially of those whose educational or other resources and attainments have been meagre.

Short in stature, with a massive head, he was not unlike his friend, Lloyd George, who visited Cliff College and spoke for him. He never preached for less than about an hour. I once stayed a week-end at Cliff, on the occasion of a conference of laymen. On the Sunday morning he concluded a devotional session at 7.0 a.m. and spoke for 50 minutes. At 10.30 a.m. in the College Chapel again we assembled for the usual service, attended by the villagers as well as students, and he preached for 60 minutes, and in the evening he preached for slightly longer. I was then in my early teens, at the Grammar School, yet never tired for a minute as I listened to his gripping exposition.

Chadwick became President of the Methodist Church, and was regarded as one of the world's greatest Biblical expositors of that time. For years he edited the weekly paper called *Joyful News*, writing the leading article for the outer page and the Editor's letter for the inside. His books (favourites of mine are *The Path of Prayer, The Way to Pentecost* and his book of sermons. *Humanity and God*), now in paperback form, are still in demand today. Utterly disciplined and dedicated to the service of God, he sought in every way to equip himself for his lectures and sermons, and withal right to the end he was the evangelist to evangelists. His study light often was burning until the early hours of the morning. It was said he went right through the English dictionary word by word, more than once, to learn their meaning. I can picture him now, walking from the main College residential quarters, up the stone steps, and entering the lecture room. The men all rise, and before be begins, they sing the hymn with which he always began his lectures:

Break Thou the bread of life,
  O Lord to me,
As Thou didst break the loaves
  Beside the sea;
Beyond the sacred page
  I seek Thee, Lord;
My spirit pants for Thee,
  O living Word.

(M.A. Lathbury)

This prayer, for such this hymn is, was always answered through his servant, Samuel Chadwick. A little man with a great faith, especially in prayer, with a great message, and a great God. No man I have ever known was a worthier sign-post to God, more faithful in pointing others to him.

Gateshead was never thought of as an attractive town, though vast improvements have been made in recent years and are continuing. The 16-storey flats, commenced in 1957, were the first in the north-east to replace so much of the drab slum property. Like Newcastle on the north bank of the Tyne, it rises steeply on the south bank – the river being spanned by five bridges. The joke about directing people to Gateshead from its dominating neighbour was understandably disliked by its citizens. In the famous vernacular it ran like this: 'Gan ower the Tyne Bridge until ye come to the end. Then ye'll look round and ye'll say to yourself "This canna be Gateshead!" But ye'll be wrang. It is!'

In the lowest part of the town, very subject to the river fogs and low in every sense (when I first knew it nearly half a century ago, police usually patrolled in couples) lies Vine Street, and in particular a mission known as 'The Vineyard'. Here a little woman has toiled for well over 50 years in the name of Christ, and has been, under God, largely responsible for transforming the area through changed lives and homes.

Sister Winifred Laver was the founder and is the leader of this well-known Vine Street Mission. She was honoured by her Majesty the Queen with the British Empire Medal in 1969. She is now over 80 years old, and is as active as ever. Recently, when asked if she rested in the afternoon, she scornfully said she hadn't come to *that* yet.

After giving her life to Christ in early years, she sought an opportunity for dedicated service. Though strongly opposed by her mother in her ambition to go as a trainee in one of the National Children's Home Bible Schools, she resolutely went forward, believing it to be the will of God. Her mother was furiously angry at this decision to 'throw away her life'. In 1911, she was put in charge of a new Girls' Home opened at Oxted in Surrey, and then sent to Frodsham in Cheshire. Tubercular glands developed, and a breakdown in health, which necessitated some months' rest, mainly in bed. She was desperately ill, but as she put it, 'I told the Lord that if He had any further work for me to do I must get well. I had never realized before that He could, if He wished, heal one's body. After several months in and out of bed I began to recover, but my doctor thought it seemed almost foolish to have gone back to work in the state I was in.'

She heard of a mission which three sets of people had tried to run and failed, leaving the place abandoned. She decided to see the Secretary of the Association which had attempted its establishment. So in 1916 she came to Vine Street, and was shown the building and the streets around it. The small mission chapel was almost derelict, windows smashed, walls broken in places, floors littered with bricks, tin cans, beer bottles, with dirt and rubbish everywhere. The houses around were old and overcrowded, children went barefoot on the cobbled streets and were very poorly clothed. She took a few days to consider it, then made her decision.

A start was made in clearing up the debris. Her first

congregation consisted of one man, eight women and a baby, and for some years it was indeed hard going. Her first step was to establish a small surgery in a room next to the Mission Hall. One early patient was a small lad, who had a very bad boil which refused to come to a head. Sister Winifred (her usual description) put on a large bread poultice and bound up his hand. Glancing down the street later, she discovered he had ripped off the bandage and had eaten the poultice.

Now the premises are transformed, a beautifully decorated and furnished Chapel has been supplemented by a large Army Hut established and made suitable for young people's work and other activities on an adjoining waste site. Young and old are provided for, and their spiritual and other needs met by what may be described as the miracle gifts of God. Printed on every Anniversary report are these words.

OUR AIMS

The Glory of God and the transforming of lives
and homes through the redemption that is in
Christ Jesus.

OUR RESOURCES

Entire dependence upon God alone for the supply of all our needs through His People.

The amazing number of *changed* lives would need a book to describe. Nor must I forget to mention in this all too inadequate description of the work the splendid service of the choirs, in the Mission and district serving other churches – note the plural! The Sisterhood and the Male Voice – Senior and Junior – choirs have each established a Tyneside reputation.

In this one-time slum area the generous support of missionary work abroad increases year by year. It is claimed that God has so guided every detail, of the financial book-keeping through all the 54 years 'that He has never allowed us to go into one month in debt. Sometimes the balance has been small, but always a balance!'

The older I get, the more reluctant I am to use the word saint in its fullest spiritual meaning, but having known Sister Winifred Laver for nearly 50 years, she has been to me a truly saintly signpost. She is the finest example I know of her Master's own words, 'Whosoever shall lose his life for my sake and the Gospel's shall find it' – or, to use her mother's expression, 'throw away her life' for Christ's sake shall reap an abundant harvest, here and hereafter.

All these signposts of mine have been people. But events also, with the people involved in them, can prove to be as significant. One example will always be for me outstanding. I had been elected from time to time by the District Synod to the Annual (then) Wesleyan Methodist Conference. It was not, however, until the Conference (now simply Methodist, after the historic *uniting* Conference in London which I attended in 1932) held at Newcastle upon Tyne in 1947 that I appeared to gain the ear of the Conference. I was asked to take part in the devotional session. Each of the three speakers had to speak on a chosen passage of scripture, mine being the words: 'That Christ may dwell in your hearts by faith'.

After I had left (I was not an elected representative that year) the President (that year Dr. W. E. Farndale) who always nominates a deputation to accompany him to the Conference of Methodists in Ireland, included my name. In retrospect, this always seemed to me the first rung on the ladder which led to the official position, that of Vice-President, which is generally described as the highest honour Methodism can bestow on a layman. Not only because I felt

I was unworthy but for several other reasons, I never had the slightest ambition in that direction. So much so that when in 1951 it became a possibility, I took positive steps to prevent it happening. But all to no avail, and I was accordingly voted on and elected Vice-President *designate*.

My friend, Dr. Sangster, who is always coming to my mind, told me he would have loved to have had me as 'stablemate', so to speak, during his own Presidency. However, we had two glorious times together when, in my designate year, I accompanied him, when he was President, to the Shetland Islands. My son was there at the time, doing a year of pre-collegiate training before going to Wesley House, Cambridge, so it is understandable that his mother accompanied me in this fascinating first visit to our most northerly isles. An SOS was received begging that one of us should go to visit Yell and Unst, as their members were so isolated from official visits and for the most part could not arrange to come to Lerwick; not without some trepidation, my wife and I agreed to go for the week-end. I took two services on the island of Yell, and then we were taken by boat across to Unst, the boatman informing us that we might be stranded for some days as in rough seas the ferry service was often suspended! Our Methodist Manse and Chapel are in one building at the extreme north of the island, and soon after our arrival the delightful young minister there took me to the back door, only a little distance from the sea and said: 'Between us standing here and the North Pole is nothing but water.' He then pointed to the left, to a small white croft, which he said was the most northerly residence in the British Isles and *occupied by a Methodist*.

The following year, when I was Vice-President and it happened to be the turn of the Channel Islands to have a visit from the Vice-President, we visited Jersey and were taken round by the Attorney General (my chairman for the evening meeting) in his car to see some of that most interesting and beautiful island. In the late afternoon he said: 'I wonder if you could spare a few minutes to call and see my aged mother? She was in your service yesterday morning, and would be so pleased to meet you personally.' We made for the south of the island, and approached a fine old manor house. 'This', he said, 'is the most southerly residence in the British Isles'. 'And,' I observed, '*occupied by a Methodist.*'

Every President and Vice-President of our Church is prayed for by thousands, so I believe, of our members and I can confirm wholeheartedly the experience of those who went before me that one does receive real and definite help in this way. It was a year crowded with events and engagements, in all of which my wife gave me invaluable and indispensable help. Keen photographer as she is, she herself took and collected from a few friends a large number of photographs which she suitably arranged and titled in an album and presented to me at the conclusion of my year. It is a full account of all our journeyings, with maps, pictures of homes and hosts and hostesses and churches visited which thus enables me to recall easily and vividly wonderful memories whenever I turn its pages. We travelled 8,000 miles by car, 5,500 by train, 680 by air and 200 by sea – a total of 14,380 miles.

One experience which came to me because of my Vice-Presidency is quite unforgettable. This was the Coronation of Queen Elizabeth II. A very small number of tickets were allocated to the Methodist Church, and the then President decided that he and the Vice-President and the Ex-President and the Ex Vice-President (which was now my position) should each be given a ticket. The result was that I had a magnificent seat in the nave near the screen and in the second row from the centre aisle. I was told that the Abbey's capacity is normally somewhere about 2,000, but for the unique event temporary galleries had been erected to quadruple the seating accommodation.

What a memorable scene it was, with all the variety of uniforms and ladies' dresses – the gallery just below the West Window resembling a vast herbaceous border in full bloom. Each one present received two books which I treasure. One, beautifully bound in red, gave the full order of service in the finest print one could conceive, the responses of the Queen being printed in red lettering. The other book gave the complete list of the processions of V.I.P. guests, officials of high state being led from the West door by Gold Stick in Waiting. Although waiting over four hours I did not feel it at all tedious, as it was so full of interest. But the figure who almost stole the show was the magnificent Queen Salote of Tonga, towering above the six (three on each side), including the Sultan of Zanzibar, who joined her processional group. With tall feathers on her head and her six feet plus inches, she was indeed regal.

The most wonderful transformation was that from the sounding of the organ and the singing of the united choirs of the Abbey and Westminster School, it immediately became a truly reverent service, and all chattering and viewing of the most colourful spectacle I have ever witnessed in my life was changed to the hushed expectancy which is the prelude to awe and true worship.

My wife and I also had the privilege, at the beginning of my year of office, as is usual, of attending a Royal Garden Party at Buckingham Palace. Alas, King George VI was unable to be present owing to illness, but the Queen – now Queen Mother – and Princesses moved among the large crowd of guests. It was interesting seeing so many well-known men and women, and it was especially made a colourful spectacle by the dresses of overseas guests.

At the conclusion of our year of office, the President and I were asked to do a recording, separately in London, at the request of the Methodist Missionary Society, in July 1952. This recording was sent to overseas Missionary centres under the title: 'What we have seen'. I will conclude this chapter with a few sentences from the manuscript I used for my recording.

'I have seen more of Methodism in these islands this year than in all the other 54 years of my life, and I am asked to tell you something of what I have seen.

'In many of the churches I have visited, I have seen a kindling of desire for more spiritual fellowship, and a longing to see the whole Church a mighty movement again, under God, to enable a revival of vital religion.

'Now when men and women *feel* like that anywhere, and turn to God, He does guide, and to an increasing number the guidance has become clear. In a sentence, it is that we need more prayer.

'Wherefore, my beloved fellow Methodists overseas, my last word to you is "pray, and keep on praying". Pray more earnestly and more faithfully for a deeper love for Christ, and, therefore, a burning passion to win others for Him. Join with others for the same purpose, for mighty things happen where two or three meet to pray in His name. "For where two or three are gathered together in my name, there am I in the midst of them". "And all things, whatsoever ye shall ask in prayer, believing, ye shall receive." Those are His words. Let us take Him at His word.

'God bless you, everyone.'

8

The Creed of an Agriculturalist

Some years ago. I was invited by the minister of the Congregational Church, Whitley Bay, Northumberland, to
address his congregation under the title 'My Faith and My
Job', which is what this chapter seeks to make clear. Let me
confess with shame that, although a practising Christian,
when I became a junior lecturer I was inclined to think of
my church life and college life in two rather separate com-
partments. In the atmosphere where, if religion is not taken
for granted, it is politely ignored, I was more inhibited as a
Christian witness, especially vocally, than I ought to have
been – *and knew it*. It was reported of one well-known
British University that several of the staff were 'Christians
on the quiet'. I am so thankful that I began to recognize my
hidden compromise and cowardice and how hypocritical it
was to sing lustily with young people in Christian rallies and
other services, 'I'm not ashamed to own my Lord', and then
lie low or miss opportunities in my job to witness to the
Christian gospel.

So I will try to describe my creed as an agriculturalist. In
my earlier days, Sir A. D. Hall, the first Director of the
world-famed Rothamsted Experimental Station – the oldest
such Station in the world – once wrote, 'There comes a time
in every thinking man's life when he has to define to himself
his view of the universe and to find some sort of faith by
which to live'. One of my own students, writing to me in the
Second World War, in one of its most critical periods, ended
his letter, 'Faith is what I want; I must have faith'. Without
it how can any life be redeemed ultimately from frustration

The Author's father and mother.

Author when President, Newcastle Free Church
eral Council, with the Lord Mayor and Rev. Dr.
old Roberts.
Photo: Newcastle Chronicle and Journal Ltd.

The Author, when Vice-President
of the Methodist Conference
(wearing M.B.E.).

The Author with two
world-famous
personalities.

▲ Pastor Martin Niemoller
Toyohiko Kagawa
(then Japan's Minister of Agriculture) ▼

and futility? The secret of a truly happy and successful life is a worthwhile faith which brings purpose, unity and meaning to our life as a whole.

In the year of my retirement (1958), the Editor of the Journal of the King's College Agricultural Society asked me to contribute an article and I chose to write under the title I have used for this chapter, and in what follows I have drawn freely from that article.

My particular creed owes much to the training and example received in a truly Christian home, but tradition began to yield to personal experience when as a youth I had to make my own decisions and in popular parlance – though a mixed metaphor when applied to farm life! – 'learn to paddle my own canoe'. What may seem a trifling yet, to me, a significant instance will illustrate this transition.

As a farm pupil I learnt much from a skilled and hard-working Irishman. On one occasion Pat delivered himself with great earnestness thus: 'Remember always to treat a stranger as a rogue until you find him to be honest.' To which I replied, 'I've been brought up to believe exactly the opposite'. I knew then that I must decide to accept or reject his advice. Of course, I have been let down occasionally over the years by the very few (such is my experience) who have refused to play the game, but I have never once regretted disregarding Pat's advice. Thus by multiplicity of personal decisions (and who can forecast which are either of little or of great importance?) we define to ourselves – to use Hall's expression – the faith by which we live; but though defined to ourselves it will surely be revealed to others in a variety of ways in our conversation and conduct. Here then are a few of the beliefs which form my creed.

1. *I believe that agriculture as a vocation affords an excellent opportunity for a full and satisfying life.* As agriculturists we are concerned with living things and the primary

E

physical needs of humanity, namely food. We study – and it is a life-time study – the mysterious and fascinating processes of nature, and the more we discover the greater our realization of what is still unknown. Nor is there any sphere in which applied science is more effective than in the oldest and most important industry in the world, to which I am privileged to belong.

Agriculture provides not only a means of livelihood – a very necessary objective for every man – but, if rightly understood, a way of life of increasing, often exciting, and certainly of enriching possibilities. No wonder one of the problems associated with the agricultural curriculum in a University – the widest surely of any faculty – is the number of subjects and the extent to which each one may be studied. Moreover the scientific agriculturalist has opportunity to avoid lop-sided development in large measure by balancing his science with the humanities.

For example, as a farmer he will be vitally concerned with human relationships in the care and management of his labour and, if he is discerning, he will know that to neglect the man inside the workman spells failure. And what a wonderful opportunity he has for the development of the culture of his inner life whilst he seeks to improve the cultivation of his land. There are assets he may build up which will not appear in any balance sheet. In my earlier days I knew a hill farmer who wrote excellent poetry in cheap exercise books as he ranged the hills. I do not think he was less a good shepherd because he reacted thus to his environment.

I recognize how important it is that a farmer should be able to judge, say, of the merits of different types of tractors or other machines in making his choice of this necessary equipment of modern farming. If he can add to that and other skills, for example, an appreciation of Constable's 'The

Hay Wain' or 'The Cornfield', I think he is a wealthier farmer, though it is wealth which is neither subject to income tax, capital gains, nor death duty. I was once taken a long motor run through what was a new agricultural district to me, and my non-agricultural host said, 'I suppose you cannot appreciate the beauty because you will be judging all the time the value of the land for farming.' How mistaken he was, for it so happens I have trained myself to be bi-focal in this respect. Very early in my career I noted and pondered the Chinese proverb, 'If you have two loaves, sell one and buy a lily'.

Wordsworth suggests an illustration of what I mean, by his character, Peter Bell:

> A primrose by a river's brim
> A yellow primrose was to him,
> And it was nothing more.

Clearly he could distinguish it from a dandelion but that was all. Had he studied in the Botany Department of a University or college, for example, the poet might have worded it thus:

> A primrose by a river's brim
> A dicotyledon was to him,
> And it was nothing more.

Chemists, or Weed Control authorities, could supply other stanzas, but I would suggest my own possibility:

> A primrose by a river's brim
> A thought of God it was to him,
> And therefore how much more.

It were tragic, surely, if a man or woman, to use Whitehead's thought, should know all about the laws of light and yet have never really seen the glory of a sunrise or the splendour of a sunset. Or again, to quote my friend Alan Fraser in *Sheep Husbandry*, 'Is the birth of a lamb any less of an unexplained mystery because the scientist calls it reproduction?' There is no reason why a farmer or an agricultural scientist should lose his soul in gaining success, though there is always that risk, if he reduces everything to the basis of material success, or loses sight of the real values of life.

The successful farmer of whom Jesus tells in the New Testament, whose outlook was dominated by the desire for larger barns, provides a warning of the perils of judging wealth by the yardstick of a bank balance. Such a life is never truly full or satisfying. Life is what one is alive to, and it can become richer and fuller so long as we retain an inquiring, exploring and wondering spirit, combined with a sense of true values.

2. *I believe that agriculture has a major contribution to make to the solution of the world's greatest problem,* namely how to establish those relationships which will enable us as nations to live together in peace. With the discovery and development of nuclear power this is the most pressing issue of our time, for if we do not learn how to live together we shall, it would seem, die together.

Food is one of the most important factors in raising the standard of living, and hunger and want a common source of that unrest from which come revolution and war. I have believed, and said repeatedly, that the only sane way to run the world is as an economic unit. Co-operation must replace what is too often truly called cut-throat competition, each nation scrambling for a place in the world's markets. Of course, in a world of intensified nationalism and with channels of distribution blocked so often by suspicion, malice and all that tends to breed war, I shall be dubbed an impractical idealist.

Yet the World Food Board, Food and Agricultural Organization, European free markets and the rest are fine trends which indicate the right direction. I cannot believe that a state of affairs is morally right which justifies the following statement from the Chairman's Review of Ranks Limited for 1956.

'As I mentioned last year good harvests are not allowed to play their normal part in reducing the price of wheat to any material extent.'

There must be more planning on an international basis of our cropping and live-stock production, in short, of our agriculture. I am aware that the problems are very complex, but I have lived long enough to see how often a complex problem has yielded to simple, direct action on the part of men of faith, vision and goodwill. At the same time this does not preclude the need for knowledge and study of the facts and consultation with experts. All through the centuries men have dreamt of the time when poverty and hunger would be banished. Not so very many years ago we used wheat for fuel for Argentine locomotives, dumped oranges into the sea, burnt coffee stocks, and kept corn off the market to bolster up an artificial price, and – irony of ironies – did these things because of so-called surpluses of food. Millions of people were living on a bare subsistence standard, and many more below this level. Even in this country, as Boyd-Orr showed, many people were living below a satisfactory standard of nutrition at that time, earlier in this twentieth century.

Wendel Wilkie, one-time candidate for the Presidency of the United States, wrote a book entitled *One World*. The title is the truth, the whole truth and nothing but the truth. It was one of my Indian students who gave me these words from the Sanskrit – ' "Is this one of our tribe or a stranger?" is the contention of the narrow-minded, but those of a noble disposition the earth itself is but one family.'

Here is a quotation (1946) from an authority in agricultural economics: 'Acute shortage of food in any major part of the world will have secondary effects in reducing wealth in the world as a whole. The more favoured peoples may choose whether they will take an immediate share of the poverty and sacrifice or wait for the incidence of secondary effects. The greater the inequality in distribution of available supplies the greater the loss of wealth and productive power, and the deeper the secondary effects of shortages. If they are willing to share some of the poverty in an immediate crisis, there will be less of it forced upon them by circumstances at a later date.'

The Apostle Paul stated the same truth nearly 2,000 years ago when he wrote: 'Who is weak and I am not weak?' America translated this same truth into action through the Marshall Plan of the post-war years; the United Nations, through its Food and Agriculture Organization, is making a great contribution, though it could be greater, and there are more voluntary agencies like Oxfam and Christian Aid than ever before in my life-time, working to this end.

It is not just distribution of surpluses that is necessary, but the supply of technical agricultural advice and equipment to enable improved production and a better balanced diet to meet the twin evils of shortage and malnutrition in the less favoured countries. It is for 'the haves' to do all in their power for 'the have-nots'; to sacrifice that others may share in a world where more than half its children are diseased and more than two-thirds of the population are still undernourished. All these recent developments – due to the greatest change I have witnessed in my life-time, namely a quickening of the social conscience – and especially the possible beneficent use of nuclear power – make me wish I were thirty years younger.

When I listen to my friend Professor Charles A. Coulson of

Oxford lecture on the peaceful use of atomic power in such possible schemes as evaporating sea water and transporting it to irrigate the great Australian desert; changing the climate of Siberia; assisting to produce new and improved varieties of crops; harvesting crops beyond the Arctic Circle, and providing power for scores of other beneficent purposes, I thrill at the possibilities of this new atomic age as applied to agriculture and to the life of man, *given a moral capacity equal to the advance in scientific knowledge.* The qualification I have italicized is all-important for, on one occasion when I heard Professor Coulson lecture, he stated that on July 18th, 1955, at West Milton, New York, Mr. Lewis L. Straus closed a giant two-way copper electric switch. Pushed one way it could start an atomic submarine propulsion moving; pushed the other way it could supply the first commercially available atomic power.

'This switch,' Straus remarked, 'is a symbol of the great dilemma of our times.'

3. *Hence the third and embracing principle of my creed is that I believe the Christian faith to be the only adequate answer to the need of man,* including that moral capacity to be fit to use the resources of science now at his disposal. Sir John Russell's closing words in his Presidential address to the British Association in Newcastle, 1949, are highly significant. 'Science can do much to overcome material difficulties ... but science can give little guidance in those great moral and spiritual problems which lie at the root of our most serious troubles today ... Science can help us best if we have a sustaining faith, a high purpose in life, and unflinching courage to pursue it.'

My humble testimony is that the Christian faith provides the finest purpose and motives for our life. It is a gift of God which may be ours if we really are willing to receive it. Time was when a student went up to the University to study 'to the glory of God' – the chapel was an integral part of the College life, whatever his subject. We should believe that *every land* is God's country, and that we are just trustees of every gift, material and spiritual, to be used for the service of God's children, irrespective of race and colour. I do not believe the distinctions 'sacred' and 'secular', but agree with a friend of mine who says there is nothing secular in this world save sin. Agriculture provides a wonderful sphere of service in which to demonstrate this great truth. The word 'cultivate' is derived from the Latin word *colere*, which according to my dictionary means 'to till, to worship'. Agriculture is an art, as well as a service and a business, and hence the words of Eric Gill are surely applicable: 'Art is collaboration with God in creation'. Surely John Ellerton, writing his hymn during the last century, proclaims the faith by which we and all men might live: 'Work shall be prayer if all be wrought as Thou wouldst have it done; and prayer by Thee inspired and taught itself with work be one.'

In 1952 I had an opportunity to declare my faith to a wider circle, when invited to read a paper to the Farmers' Club in London on the subject of 'Agricultural Education'. After a lengthy historical survey of the development of agricultural education and the growing appreciation of its value, I concluded in terms which I believe are as relevant now as then.

'In all our plans and policies for agricultural education we should keep clearly in mind that we are educating persons for life. In short, agricultural education has to do with the education of an agriculturalist, and is not just a system of technical instruction for an industry. If this is accepted as the basic principle, there are several implications in seeking to improve our agricultural education.

'The first of these is that we should remember that the noun is more important than the adjective, and that it is easy to stress the word "agricultural" so that education becomes simply a means to the end that farming may be made more profitable. If in using the word "profitable" we include the harvest of the mind and soul, or those assets and rewards which can never be tabulated in annual balance sheets, then I am quite happy to use that word; but all too often agricultural education has been judged solely on its efficiency in gaining more monetary profit.

'I do not question for a moment the very great importance of doing all possible by the training of agriculturalists in sound management of their business to enable maximum production of food, especially in a world that needs all we can produce, and we literally cannot afford to neglect the money side of the farming business. I am not forgetful of the very difficult times experienced by farmers between the two wars, or of many in these days, and the consequent deterioration in value to the nation of its most important material asset, namely, the land. Yet the inner satisfactions of those who cultivate the land come from other things and are enjoyed more fully when money takes second place. Education worthy of the name inspires man with the highest ideals, and of these the ideal of service should be supreme. In practical farming enterprise I am sure the word attributed, I think, to Burne-Jones, 'Making the most of your best for the sake of others', in the long run is a sounder incentive than what is commonly termed the "profit motive".

'The second implication is the need for giving all who are engaged in agriculture opportunities for the right kind of education. In view of the great variety of employment in agriculture, no one suggests that it is an easy matter to achieve a comprehensive plan, but that should be our constant aim. Education is that training, instruction and guidance by example as well as precept, which enables persons to learn how to think, feel and act rightly and continuously (seeing that we never truly 'finish' our education) in the sphere of life in which they find their vocation.

'The third implication is the need for more attention to the study of human relationships. Applied psychology may be of some value for those who will be called to manage staff on a farm, teach in a farm institute, or act as advisers to the farming community; but the education of the future must, I feel, deal with the world problems of our age at a deeper level, and this brings me to my final consideration.

'Since I began teaching, over thirty years ago, there have been many significant changes, two of which I shall mention; one is a source of encouragement – the other a challenge. The first is the growing appreciation in the farming community of agricultural education. Earlier in this paper I quoted from an address by Professor T. H. Middleton at the beginning of the century. In that same address he used the following words: "If we judge by actions rather than by words, not five farmers in fifty have any faith in the practical benefits of education either for themselves or their sons ... the truth is the desire for education is lacking."

'To some extent, no doubt, those responsible for education and the planning of the courses were to blame, but in the shorter period covered by my experience I have found a very big change for the better in the attitude of farmers to agricultural education and scientific research.

'The other change, which to me is the more revolutionary, is that we have all become, of necessity, more world-minded, because the modern world is a neighbourhood though tragically lacking at present in good neighbourly relationship. The great need of our world at this time is for a strong faith and a sense of guidance such as will enable men and women of every nation to realize the unity of mankind, for which, together with security, I believe our age is in travail. I have great confidence in agriculturalists being able to set an example of world unity, for already, as primary producers, they have sought to secure closer co-operation. Lord Boyd-Orr's vision of an effective World Food Board we shall learn, sooner or later, is the only way to sanity in a world where isolationism and selfish narrow nationalism or self-sufficiency are illusions.

'Agricultural education, therefore, should help to make possible, directly or indirectly, the formation of a sound creed, and for my own part I doubt if there is such a person as a creedless farmer. It is, however, important to get the right creed and the most stable and valuable foundation, I believe, is a sound religious faith. Like the man who, when questioned by a friend why he devoted much time and energy to physical exercises, replied, "Well, one must keep fit," which drew the further question from his friend, namely, "Fit for what?"

'I may be accused of mixing the studies of divinity and agriculture. If so, I make no apology, for I affirm it is an excellent mixture. No man could wish for a higher vocation than the study of the cultivation of the soil and the soul. I do not believe, with Wells, Shaw and Bertrand Russell, that education in the commonly accepted meaning of the word together with more intelligence, can save the world – and heaven pity us if in these days we cannot see it needs saving. The Christian faith affirms our need of a power other than our own to effect that radical change in human nature which makes possible new men. Yet education of the right kind has its part to play in that enlightenment which may be the prelude to that change, and to all the changes, personal and social, which should issue from it. In short, I'm emphasizing the value and need of a closer link between learning and living, and especially of learning how to live in peace together.

'Hence, I conclude that education, including – or, as I would say, especially – agricultural education, can make its maximum contribution to the welfare of life only when it seeks in every possible way to help men and women of the land everywhere to understand the meaning of the truth of the words on the Royal Exchange, London, "The earth is the Lord's and the fullness thereof", and to possess as the motive for their daily work the injuncton of nineteen centuries ago, "Whatsoever ye do, do all to the glory of God." For only then shall men know the truth, that though some must be subordinate to others, none need feel inferior.'

It has been my experience that if in natural sequence in the subject dealt with, and stated simply and sincerely, the expression of one's faith and creed, so far from being resented, is received kindly and with understanding, even by any who do not accept it.

9

A Changed and Changing World

> '*If anybody had predicted 30 years ago the develop-
> ments we now take for granted, he would have been
> dismissed as a complete madman.*'
> The Rt. Hon. Anthony Wedgwood Benn, M.P.

It seems a far cry from the world of the pony-trap of my
early days to travelling to the moon in the seventies. I once
wrote out a list, beginning with a postcard and ending with a
foolscap sheet, of the things my grandfather – farming in
Yorkshire last century – never missed because he never knew
them. No telephones, tanks, jet planes, motor cars, sound
radio, television, computers, or votes for women, overtime or
holiday rates of pay for his farm workers ... and so I might
go on for the remainder of this chapter.

In my life-time there have been more changes in that most
conservative industry, agriculture, than in the previous 2,000
years. I recall visiting a farm early in the Second World War
in Northumberland and pausing to watch a new combine
(the first to reach Northumberland country in 1940) at work.
'Would you like to hop up with me?' was the invitation of
the driver, eagerly accepted. On the further side of the field
he pointed out a cottage where his grandmother lived. She
had seen corn harvested in this field by sickle and gathered
into bundles (as in the days of Ruth and Boaz in the Old
Testament): then by Irishmen using 20 scythes working in
wonderful rhythm, with women following to gather, tie with

straw, and bunch into sheaves; then with the manual
(machine) reaper and the same hand-tying (the most back-
aching farm job I have ever experienced); then with the self-
binder, which cut the corn, tied it with string, throwing out
the sheaves which were subsequently gathered by hand
and erected into stooks. 'Now,' said my friend on the combine, 'she is watching this machine cut, thresh and collect
the grain in one operation, and she thinks "it is of the
devil!" '.

I do not subscribe entirely to the line of the well-known
hymn which reads, 'Change and decay in all around I see',
though I often repeat the prayer, 'O Thou who changest
not, abide with me.' I well remember a popular item in
sound broadcasting of many years ago. A hansom cab driver,
talking to his horse, was recalling former days, and his oft-
repeated phrase was, 'It isn't everything that changes,
changes for the good.' He was right, and lowering standards
of honesty, attitudes to work, decline in true patriotism and
therefore community feeling and thought for others as well
as the increase in violence and vandalism, make understandable what my doctor said recently, when referring to a
despicable act of thieving, 'I don't know what the world is
coming to nowadays.'

In things agricultural it is interesting to note not a few
returns to older practices and long-established principles.
For example, the 'slurry' problem (liquid and solid excreta
and water used on concrete floors) to date seems to get no
further than a return to the traditional making of more
farmyard manure. Also sound rotational cropping for areas
over-cropped with corn is coming back into its own, as well
as mixed farming being safer as we go into the Common
Market.

Yet there are changes which are for the good, as compared
with the earlier days. I have lived under six Sovereigns, and

I can recall standing with my father beside a large tub from which he was ladling soup, with a clothes basket beside it from which he was handing out chunks of bread to poor women clutched by children, ill-clad, with no shoes on their feet. In those days no State assiistance, dole, or old age pensions existed, and in large factories men were laid off work or discharged from time to time. Redundancy payments were a pipe-dream, if they were dreamed of at all!

As I have said, the greatest change for the good I have seen is the quickening of the social conscience and the removal of dire poverty through the adoption of a Welfare State. The National Health Service has its critics, and shortage of doctors has meant in many cases the passing of the 'family doctor', but the benefits of the best known treatment for each and all, regardless of expense, far outweigh the disadvantages and I for one am grateful for all my wife and I have received in this way. Years ago, my own brother-in-law, who used to visit the U.S.A. regularly, purchasing tobacco leaf for his firm, was once a hospital case there, and before he got home his illness had cost him £1,000.

Many changes took place, especially in the Second World War, not least the disappearance of the word 'dole' and the adoption of at least the objective of full employment. Some criticize now the swing of the pendulum whereby today it is possible for some to stay away from work and receive as much, if not a little more, than if employed but I am thankful for better nourished children and the alleviation of real poverty by State and local authorities. In my own city hundreds of slum houses have been demolished and replaced by sky-scraper flats in a green setting and newly planted trees as well as some of the older, well-constructed houses being reconstructed into useful flats. But there still remains a great and urgent need for more houses.

I love my country, and pray and strive for it to be in the

van of spiritual and moral leadership for the sake of the world of nations. As Sir Arthur Bryant, the historian wrote in *The Lion and the Unicorn*:

'For England is a Christian land, and only by contemplation of her long Christian history can one comprehend her.'

R. F. Delderfield, the best-seller writer, urges more positive action by leading churchmen.

'They might begin by pointing out that such civilization as we possess in these islands stems almost entirely from the Gospel the early Christian missionaries brought here some fifteen centuries ago.'

Alas, the patriotism of peace is so much poorer than the patriotism of war when in the latter we worked and sacrificed for the *common* good.

A one-time colleague said to me not long ago: 'You had the best days of University life'. I do not share this pessimistic note, though there are features in student unrest which may give serious concern. Disquietude can lead, if rightly handled, to better things; and protest of the right kind with constructive ideas can result in genuine improvement and progress. The scriptural principle is still relevant, 'Overcome evil with good'. So much criticism is negative. To some people a battle is more exciting than building, and it is easier to destroy than to construct. I believe there are as many fine young people in our country today as ever there have been. It is a minority, given too much press and TV publicity, which give to many people a wrong impression of modern youth.

In *The Times* for October 15th, 1970, I found a full-page advertisement with the heading in large type: 'The way the young people of Northern Ireland are acting should be enough to make you stop and think.' Then came the following: 'Our young people are not all roaming the streets.

For the most part the young people of Northern Ireland are primarily concerned with building a future for themselves.'

I think, also, of several of my friends and past students who have served under Voluntary Service Overseas, seeking in this way to fulfil the exhortation of John Wesley, 'Go not to those who need you but to those who need you most.' Christian Aid, Oxfam, and so many other voluntary agencies are doing splendid service to make possible a Welfare World. I think in this connection of a past student called Pamela Goode. After taking an honours degree in Agricultural Botany she was led to dedicate her life, gifts and training to the glory of God. This led to a call of God to go out and work in Uganda. There she worked at a High School where a Farm Diet Scheme was initiated in 1955, largely pioneered by the activity and interest of Sir Robert Hutchinson, then Director of the Empire Cotton Growing Corporation Research Station. Pamela, who had always been keen on practical farming, was given charge of the small farm brought into cultivation from the dense cover of elephant grass. The scheme was to encourage the growth of more protein crops, and the girls in the School were taught how to use and blend them with other foods to provide a more balanced human diet. She found tremendous difficulties and at times she almost despaired, but she remained faithful to her call, enlarged the area, and cultivated and increased the number of livestock, including a dairy herd. Incidentally, I found it interesting that the School was maintained by the Church Missionary Society, which is Anglican. Pamela is a Methodist, and Sir Robert Hutchinson, I believe, a Quaker. This is Christian unity in practice in the service of God's children.

I confess to a nostalgic feeling concerning the days when I began to learn the practice of farming. The smell of the

F

upturned furrow, guiding the plough drawn by two magnificent Shire horses, and at the end of the day making them comfortable for the night, had something which the modern tractor lacks. Moreover, there was no fear of any physical trouble resulting from too much sitting and too little walking, as in some forms of farm mechanization. Ruby, Jack, Daisy, and Boxer, to recall just four names after 60 years, with their whinneying greeting when one entered the stable very early in the morning, provided a closer human link than does a combine or, to anticipate, say a press-button remote-control tractor.

Even more, I cannot feel happy about some forms of agricultural production developing today. I suppose I would be regarded as a reactionary in that I much prefer 'free range' eggs, and chicken or meat produced without the aid of antibiotics. I was far from happy when inspecting a modern fattening pig house, with its controlled temperature, lighting, and what I felt was overcrowding. When the Principal of the College unlocked the door of this expensive structure and ushered me in, I felt I was in a prison and inspecting the inmates of the cells. When I discussed with him one or two disease troubles already being experienced, his reply was, 'Oh we give them this and that to correct such things, and science will provide all the antidotes'. It seemed to me a dangerous 'interference with nature'. I next went into the dim-lighted poultry house, with its hundreds of birds in batteries, obviously unnaturally scared of a stranger like myself. Later, I saw the chicken unit, where they are reared and never see the light of God's sunshine.

I know the arguments for more and cheaper food for the masses, but more often than not the primary motive is more profit and the effect of increasing competition, although the vast majority of farmers have the highest regard for their animals, as I know. 'Are we cashing in on cruelty?' the Daily

Mirror survey report had for its heading. Food can be too cheap, and 'subsidy' is rightly, I think, not a word popular with farmers. A nation (to quote 1971 figures) that spends in a year a total of £6,371 millions on alcoholic liquor, tobacco and gambling, can afford farming support and to pay more for the actual cost of home-produced food, without undue hardship in general, so long as unfair burdens do not fall on low income groups. 'I am sure no farmer wants his salvation in the form of a "dole slip" – he'd surely prefer to get it all from the market as a fair return from a fair effort.' (*Farmer* editorial, November 1970.) I have seen it reported in 1970 that we are spending a smaller proportion on food today. Ten years ago it was a third of our income, now it is barely one-fifth.

I guard as vigorously as I can with advancing years against the mental rigidity and conservatism which is not open to consider change and new ideas. Yet it is interesting to observe how premature scapping of the old or traditional is not always in the end to the advantage of the farmer. An experiment may be different when translated into experience. Scientists are not infallible guides. The adoption of artificial insemination produced spectacular results in raising average milk production, but I doubt if its full repercussions were ever investigated as fully as they merited by scientists. The effect, too, on those who look after farm animals of some methods of factory farming is given scant thought. In 1956, when I was in the U.S.A., I visited an experimental farm in North Carolina and noted with surprise that a new cow byre was being constructed in place of the more modern parlour system, and was told, 'We think we can do better with a return to the byre system for the dairy herd.'

Take poultry as another example. There is a certain farm from which I purchase supplies. This is a bleak, wind-swept, exposed hill farm situated over 1,000 feet above sea level, with ordinary free-range poultry houses, the shelter being provided by the stone walls of the field, common to Northumberland. The eggs are of the highest quality and flavour. The flock is replenished by purchased pullets which are kept for two years – not the one year which is all the battery pullets can stand. I understand from the farmer's wife that the hens rarely use the shelter of the poultry house during the day, even in winter. What a contrast to looking at hundreds of birds herded in cages in subdued artificial lighting! Foxes I know are a menace to the free range poultry flocks, but I believe farmers could be left to solve this problem as they do stray dog killers rather than preserving foxes for blood sport.

There is much wisdom in what Mr. Tristram Beresford wrote under the title 'As the Farmer Sees It' in *The Countryman*. 'It seems that there is a line, not clearly drawn, beyond which efficiency shades off into exploitation; and if exploitation is mistaken for efficiency, then efficiency is lethal.' If farming interferes with nature, then nature is sure to send in the bill in the form of disease and other troubles.

Whilst Rachel Carson's *Silent Spring*, and Ruth Harrison's *Animal Machines*, and Elspeth Huxley's *Brave New Victuals* may be criticized, I honour these women writers for emphasizing that there can be unwise interference with nature and insufficiently considered actions. Equally, I welcome the challenge of the Year of Conservation (1970) and the splendid work being done, including that by young people, to restore the waste places and make beautiful or useful the ugly and despoilt. I saw a vision of this possibility when many years ago slag colliery waste land and pit heaps were planted with trees; for example, the road approaching the Durham County Farm at Houghall. After 40 years, there is ample evidence of the regeneration of indigenous oak. We are told in Genesis to subdue nature, not destroy it, either by exploitation or pollution.

I have lived to see the day when alcoholic drinking is recognized as a potential danger and we are counselled in these days of breathalizers and blood tests: 'If you drink don't drive, and if you drive don't drink.' Many years ago in a Youth Meeting, during the discussion a young man asked me why Methodism, which as he rightly said has one Sunday a year called Temperance (now Christian Citizenship) Sunday, said nothing about the evil of excessive smoking. Nowadays, in doctors' surgeries and public advertisements I see grim warnings of this smoking habit. At a bus station in Newcastle I noticed seven posters in a row depicting a lot of cigarette ends and bearing the inscription, 'The best tip, give it up. Cigarettes harm your health.' According to one estimate the habit causes a tenth of all deaths.

I shall be surprised if some critic of this book does not dub me a temperance fanatic, or charge me with excessive emphasis on the evil of alcoholism, from which so many other evils derive – but is it really possible to exaggerate it? In the third volume of Cecil Robert's most interesting autobiography *The Bright Twenties*, I read, 'When the Japanese swooped down on the American Fleet in Pearl Harbour, Honolulu, at 7.55 a.m. on Sunday December 7th, 1941, they knew that the crews were sleeping off the effects of their customary Saturday night "binge".' In November 1970 our daily newspaper, the *Newcastle Journal*, had a headline on the front page of Sir Gerald Nabarro's jibe at the North – 'Booze first, kids later'. In an article commenting on this remark in the House of Commons next day, the writer (although obviously in no sense pro-Nabarro, for his article is headed 'Sir Gerald is right for once') stated that in the North of England we spend more on alcohol and tobacco than any other part of Britain, although our average weekly income is the second lowest, and we spend less on food than anywhere else in the country. He ends the article, 'But the more depressing side of the picture is that the "alcoholism explosion" may be costing the nation £250 million a year in absenteeism and in shoddy work.' From the *Newcastle Journal* of November 28th, 1970, comes this: 'Britain has more than 300,000 alcoholics. And over the past three years there has been a sharp increase in addiction to drink in the 18-25 age group.'

In my own University some subjects have been given new titles: What I taught under 'Crop Husbandry' is now 'Crop Production', and 'Animal Production' replaces 'Animal Husbandry'. The change is not without some significance, for in my humble judgment Husbandry is the better word, for it implies all the care and attention to an animal which we used to embody in 'stockmanship' – a good shepherd and a fine stockman. I am not suggesting that such craftsmen – as indeed they are – are not found on farms today, but mechanization and the word efficiency need careful consideration when measuring human values. I still hold – despite the opposition of some pundits – that farming is a life as well as a means of making a livelihood. I doubt, for example, if any hill farmer, poor as are the financial returns for this type of farming, would doubt that statement. It is, of course, primarily a business, but it need not be a soul-impoverishing industry, as is not a remote possibility in a scientific machine age.

Sir Josiah Stamp's published lectures bear the significant title, *The Christian Ethic as an Economic Factor,* and he declares that this factor is much neglected by economists. The ethics of Christianity are a greater need now, so I believe, than in any age of history. In all our problems of conservation, pollution, world trade, food for a hungry world, that need is fundamental, for in the end the heart of every problem, as has been said, is 'the problem of the human heart', and if I understand Christianity at all, I affirm that the essential purpose of the Gospel is to deal with that fundamental problem. Only the full-orbed Gospel, full acceptance of the principles and practice arising from personal acceptance of a living faith in Christ, can lead the way to the establishment of what is the Kingdom of God, and for which millions pray daily: 'Thy Kingdom come, Thy will be done on earth, as it is in heaven.' We need a book on *Spiritual Law in the Natural World*.

The heart of the Gospel and the needs of the heart of man possess an unchanging essence. In all our emphasis on change there are many things which have not changed – day and night, the ebb and flow of the tide, the seasons as they come and go, the laws which have to be studied to effect a journey to and upon the moon. Men still need peace of mind, worthwhile purpose, and power to strive for the best values. They still cry and shout, triumph and fail, sin and know remorse, and in their best moments know Paul's experience and diagnosis of the human heart, 'The wish is there but not the power of doing what is right' (Moffatt's translation). I question the intelligence of a person who thinks the world has no need of salvation, not only from poverty, war, racial strife and other vast problems and conflicts, but fundamentally as persons from sin, selfishness, indifference, materialism and other perverse elements in human nature.

This leads me to the changes I have witnessed in the Church in my life-time. A disunited church can never be the channel of God's power. A united Christian Church, caring, sharing, daring and redeeming, would not only meet the challenge of Communism or atheistic secularism but the full needs, physical and spiritual, of all men everywhere.

Up to this century the Church was constantly being fragmented, but in my life-time the movement has been reversed and there is a slow but, I believe, sure movement of coming together again. In open air work in The Bigg Market, Newcastle, and elsewhere, I constantly got the question "Why all the separate denominations?" – and whilst I could say that God had ruled and over-ruled all such disputes, mistakes and failures to the end that His purpose might be fulfilled, I *knew* how inadequate was the answer in *the twentieth century*, with its urgent need of universal brotherhood. In the early years of the Second World War (1940), my wife and I invited to our home the Ministers and Pastors of all the churches in our area of the West End of Newcastle. 26 out of a possible 32 met for tea, and after prayer and full discussion the West End Christian Forward Movement was formed, with the Vicar of Benwell Parish Church and my own Minister of Dilston Road Methodist Church as leaders, and the Rev. R. Cameron and myself were elected Secretaries. We arranged united services for worship in the various churches, and systematic house-to-house visitations (in couples of lay members of different churches), meeting people personally for a talk and leaving behind a leaflet, which included the aims of the movement.

One person receiving this leaflet and reading the list of thirty-eight churches on the back of it said, 'But I thought all these Churches were jealous of one another.' The movement eventually came to an end, partly because of Anglo-Catholics who said we were 'starting too far down the course', but it was the forerunner of the formation not long afterwards of the Newcastle Council of Churches for United Christian Action.

Today, my own church, Dilston Road Methodist, is working on the closest terms with the Anglican Church known as St. James and St. Basil. The Vicar, curates and lay-readers are printed in our Methodist Circuit plan, published quarterly, giving the Sunday appointments for the preachers at our 12 Methodist Churches and at St. James and St. Basil's. We have united services at each church of Holy Communion, and have joined in united house group meetings, joint retreats, and progress continues in further developments of Christian fellowship. An important example is preparation for membership and confirmation on a joint basis, and in 1972 a united service for the young people received and confirmed in which the Assistant Bishop of Newcastle diocese and Rev. J. Skidmore B.A. of our Methodist Church took the leading part and afterwards the large congregation of Methodists and Anglicans joined in Holy Communion. As I near the frontier between time and eternity I feel increasingly the need for more rapid progress at the grass roots of this desirable and most needful unity. For many years I have advocated the printing on our public notice boards 'The Church in England' (and if necessary Anglican, Baptist, etc. in brackets afterwards).

That is why, with my nine grandchildren in mind and what the world will be like in this rapidly changing world, I spoke to the Methodist Conference of 1969 in favour of the Scheme for Re-uniting with the Church of England, and voted for it.

I do not think our Lord ever intended exclusiveness of any of His followers at what is the Lord's Table, the Last Supper or Eucharist. After all, the Church exists not for perfect people but for sinners who desire to be perfected by His grace, and at the First (which we call the Last) Supper there were present one who betrayed Him, another who denied Him – is there any essential difference? – and in the crisis that followed St. Mark tells us, 'And they all forsook Him and fled', though all but one returned to make a new beginning and form His Church.

The challenging and timely topic of the 1970 address of the President of the British Association, namely 'Time to

Think', was certainly relevant to our need today. 'The nub of our problem today is fantastically rapid technological advance coupled with relatively slow social progress', declared Lord Trumpington, Master of Christ's College, Cambridge. Surely it is moral progress, the product of greater spiritual progress, which is the weakness. My disappointment was that no mention of God was made in the address, but only of 'informed public opinion' as the hope of 'making of correct choices'. Great and wonderful as are the discoveries of science, and beneficial indeed as are many of the technological applications, my deepest conviction in this changing world is that only in re-discovery of the reality of God and spiritual revival shall we find the way to a better world for the rising generation.

I agree with my fellow Methodist, Professor Sir Herbert Butterfield, in the principle he stated, which is rightly oft-quoted, 'Hold to Christ and for the rest be totally uncommitted', but I am sure the Master of Peterhouse College, Cambridge, realizes that to hold to Christ is to be committed to 'The Way, the Truth and the Life', and I often wish he would expound more fully what he feels is involved in his now famous dictum.

God's purpose can therefore, I believe, be summarized as follows:–

1. God intended the world to be run as an economic unit. We are all stewards (the New Testament word) or trustees for God of all His gifts for all His children.

2. There is no longer any abiding security for any nation in armaments. I can no longer distinguish between offensive and defensive weapons.

3. God 'hath made of one blood all nations of men for to dwell on all the face of the earth' (Acts 17: 26). Racialism and all such barriers between God's children are both stupid and sinful.

The common temptation every individual has to face is insidious and subtle. One tells oneself there is so little, if anything, the individual can do to bring about a better world or help to solve the vast, complex problems of the world of today. Always, when so tempted, I recall the words of that political authority, F. D. Roosevelt, one-time President of the U.S.A.: 'Public opinion is created by less than 5 per cent of the population'; and alongside this statement that of Professor Toynbee: 'All progress is in response to challenge.' Hence my common prayer these days is, 'Lord I have faith, help me where faith falls short' Mark 9: 24 (N.E.B.).

In the *Spectator* for October 17th, 1970, under 'Medicine', there was published an article on the common problem of disease of our age, namely fear or anxiety. 'By all logical standards this should be a golden, carefree age,' writes John Rowland Wilson, yet 'Anxiety is at the root of the vast array of so-called "functional" ailments that make up about half a general practitioner's work.' He concludes his article with these words: 'The only remedy for anxiety is a restoration of self-confidence, a sense of proportion, a calmer, more dignified acceptance of life's inevitable ups and downs. *Which I suppose some of us at least used to get from religion, in those far-off days when it was fashionable.*' (The italics are mine.)

I do believe – despite the widespread apathy and materialism at home and abroad today – that more and more will return to Him who said 'Come unto me . . . and I will give you rest . . . Learn of me and ye shall find rest.' Not the rest or peace of selfish ease, but of purposeful, righteous activity in service for others and for God.

10

Shortening Years and
Lengthening Horizons

'Now you will be living on borrowed time'
(My sister, when I reached my 70th birthday)

I decided, after much prayer, to choose the earlier retirement
date of 60. There was no reason on the ground of health but
only a desire for more time and freedom to devote my remaining years to writing, preaching and personal coun-
selling. I have worked hard all my life, and have loved work,
so I did not think of retirement as more leisure.

Each winter since 1957 I have given occasional single
evening lectures at the Agricultural Colleges of Northumberland, Durham and Cumberland and Westmorland.
The subject for such lectures must be 'off the beaten track' of
the curriculum, and more often than not I have chosen
'Christianity and Agriculture' and have enjoyed most
interesting, prolonged discussion, including a great variety of
questions on this subject and its various aspects. There are
some splendid young people in the rising generation who
never receive the publicity (and they don't want it) that some
wayward youth receive in these press 'headlines' days. Addresses at Schools, Colleges and Industrial and other Christian groups have given me other welcome opportunities of
sharing my experience and witness of the Christian faith.

I have often prayed John Wesley's prayer: 'Lord, let me
not live to be useless'. Yet there are times when such interests
have to be suspended. I have had a total of about nine oper-

ations, some major, involving months in hospital. I would not have chosen such experiences of pain and suffering but, looking back, I have realized again and again the blessing God brought to me in such trials. The Apostle Paul uses the words 'comforted to comfort'. I used to visit friends in hospital with sincere sympathy and prayerful thoughts for them but limited to a certain extent by the viewpoint of a vertical perspective, but since my own experiences as a patient I am able to feel with them in a much deeper way what it means to lie in a horizontal position. No less do I appreciate with abiding gratitude hospital medical, and nursing ancillary staff.

Hence I can humbly claim that I have been made able better to understand what others suffer through bereavement, illness and physical handicap because I have known at first hand, what it is to mourn or to be 'laid aside'. These last two words are from the personal commitment a Methodist makes who attends on the first Sunday of the year what is known as the Covenant Service. The concluding paragraphs which the congregation repeat are well worth quoting:

> 'I am no longer my own, but Thine. Put me to what Thou wilt, rank me with whom Thou wilt; put me to doing, put me to suffering; let me be employed for Thee or laid aside for thee, exalted for Thee, or brought low for Thee; let me be full, let me be empty; let me have all things, let me have nothing; I freely and heartily yield all things to Thy pleasure and disposal. And now, O glorious and blessed God, Father, Son and Holy Spirit, Thou art mine and I am Thine. So be it. And the covenant which I have made on earth, let it be ratified in heaven. Amen.'

I repeated these words at the service on January 4th, 1970,

and prayed that I might really mean them – for nothing is easier than to repeat creeds and liturgical prayers and mean little by them – and on January 13th was struck down by a coronary thrombosis. Recovery, I was informed by the medical specialist, was a six months' job for a man of my age. Having experienced such an active life, this seemed a long time of enforced rest, but it provided the opportunity denied in days of crowded diaries of engagements to sit back and tackle this book of reminiscences. Thankfully, I am now (1973) preaching and speaking again.

Happiness in retirement is not, however, a matter only of many interests, though these play their part. It is to me much more dependent on fellowship and friendship. A. G. Street is quoted by his daughter, Pamela Street, in her delightful book, *My Father*, as saying: 'In looking back on my life, the bulk of the worthwhile things in it are connected with friendship.' How true, as I can wholeheartedly confirm.

When I retired, I received a handsome cheque from the College Agricultural Society, a Rolex watch from my colleagues, a television set and a walking stick given to me by the farm workers at Cockle Park. To this I must add a present which had (to me) a rather dramatic sequel.

'On the eve of my retirement, some half dozen of the senior students of the School of Agriculture manoeuvred me through a door into a room packed with students. Within a few minutes, I was listening to a prepared short speech and being presented with a beautiful standard reading lamp, finely inscribed. I was so taken aback that I was at a loss for words. To gain a few moments, I told them it reminded me of my last day at school, and my headmaster's words, 'If you'll keep it up, you'll get there'. 'If by "get there",' I said, 'he meant I should make a lot of friends, he was right, for I have become a millionaire in friendship.'

Next day, when on my way home for lunch along the Haymarket, I happened to glance at the newspaper posters. One of them, Newcastle's daily newspaper, read:

'KINGS' MILLIONAIRE

PROFESSOR.

Story and picture.'

My first thoughts were that one of our Kings' College Professors had been left a fortune by a relation in Australia or the U.S.A. and, being interested to know, went in and bought a copy. I discovered that someone must have reported my words about friendship. It never entered my head that anything about this private, homely incident would get into the press and that I should strike the headlines for the first and last time! 'His friends are legion,' wrote Dr. Sangster in his article in the *Methodist Recorder* when I became Vice-President.

How true it is that we should count a man's wealth by the number of his real friendships! You live in people more than in things or places, and now I have retired I value more than ever fellowship and friends. I have many friends who do not profess the Christian faith, but my own experience is that the finest of all are Christian friends. I for one would not deny that you can be a good workman, a good parent, a good citizen and a good friend without Christ, but I would still hold that you cannot realize your highest potential in any of these vocations until you can declare, as the Apostle Paul wrote: 'Life means Christ to me.' As a small boy. I used to sing in the Sunday School, 'The best friend to have is Jesus' and 'What a friend we have in Jesus.' A lifetime's experience confirms the truth of these words. The highest honour we can have is to become a friend of Jesus. 'Ye are my friends,' He said to His disciples. He thanked God for them in His

prayers. In His last prayer for them He said: 'They belonged
to you and you gave them to me' (John 17: 6. *Today's English Version*); and in the same version (Luke 22, 28), he says:
'You have stayed with me all through my trials.'

How swiftly the years have passed, and never more so
than the last decade.

> *When as a child I laughed and wept,*
> > *Time crept;*
> *When as a youth I thought and talked,*
> > *Time walked;*
> *When I became a full grown man,*
> > *Time ran;*
> *When elder still I grew,*
> > *Time flew;*
> *Soon I will find, in passing on,*
> > *Time gone.*

In his book *The Island*, Ronald Lockey writes: 'The soul
of a young man yearns for the horizons beyond experience.'
Yes, but it is also true of one who may be old in years but
young in heart. To the Christian, it is always true that the
best is yet to be, and whilst eager to live as long as possible
here on earth, he should be ready for the call whenever it
comes.

In the meantime, I repeat how blessed is God's gift of
friends, both young and old, strengthening, enriching, and
comforting us in our faith in God's loving purpose. 'With all
these witnesses to our faith around us like a cloud', says the
writer of the Epistle to the Hebrews, according to the N.E.B.
translation, but in the *Today's English Version* it reads: 'We
have this large crowd of witnesses around us.' So I look forward to my daily post, and especially at Christmas time, and
as I look at the cards and read the greetings, the face and life

of the sender becomes real to me. One example must suffice. One night in 1932 a girl came forward in a mission I was conducting on Tyneside to give her life to Christ. I told her and the group of young people with her that if in the future they would like to assure me that they were still faithful and loyal to their decision, three letters would suffice, namely S.W.J. ('Satisfied with Jesus'). *Every year since* I have received her Christmas card, always bearing the letters 'S.W.J.', preceded in some years by the words 'More and more'. I have never seen her since that first meeting so long ago.

As time passes, heaven becomes more and more 'home to our hearts' (in the words of a prayer in the funeral service) as, one by one, loved ones are called to our eternal home. I like to think of such friends helping our Lord to prepare the place He promised to all who trust and love Him. The closer we keep to Him the nearer we are to each other, for those we love who depart this life in His faith are for ever with us because they are for ever with Him. I think now of one such friend.

Dr. W. E. Sangster was guest in our home for the Methodist Conference in Newcastle in 1958, and it was during that week he received confirmation from his London consultant that he had contracted the disease called muscular atrophy, for which there was no known cure; he knew that in consequence his days were definitely numbered. He had been feeling ill for some time, but gallantly discharged his responsibilities in the Conference. On the Sunday morning however, his Conference-appointed service at Sunderland was taken by the Rev. Dr. Harold Roberts. After lunch that day he requested that he might have my summerhouse to himself the whole afternoon that he might face the challenge, at 58 years of age, of his life being cut short. I was told to bring him a cup of tea at 4 p.m., and to see he was not disturbed till then. When I took him his tea there was a silence I shall never forget, and then I felt guided by God to speak.

'Will, you would like to preach tonight, wouldn't you?'

'I would give my right arm to do so, Cecil' was his immediate response. 'But it rests with you. Bring the notes of a sermon in your pocket, take the service up to the hymn before the sermon, and I will tell you then, but not before, if I can preach.'

With prophetic insight, Dr. Arthur Hill of Ipswich (the unofficial honorary physician friend to the Methodist Conference) said,

'Let him attempt it. I'll be to hand in the service if anything happens. Who knows, it might be the last time he can preach.'

Half way through the all-important hymn, Dr. Sangster stepped forward.

'I'll preach,' he whispered.

He spoke powerful words on the Perils of Procrastination (Felix to Paul – 'When I find it convenient I will send for you again', Acts 24: 25 N.E.B.). After 20-25 minutes his voice began to thicken (a symptom of his trouble), and he wisely brought his sermon to a close and gave out the last hymn. In the second verse he stepped back.

'Shall I make an appeal?' he whispered.

'I cannot decide that, Will', was my immediate reaction. He resumed his place at the platform desk, then in the last verse turned back to me again and said just three words with great intensity.

'You *must* say'.

'Well then', I replied, 'I would if I were you.'

And two young men and a young lady in their twenties stood up in silent response to his invitation to give their lives to Christ.

Eleven years later, I was at that church again. I ascertained that of the young men concerned, one was a fully accredited local preacher, while the other held several offices including Sunday School Superintendent; the young lady was now in London and, it was believed, true to her vow made that Sunday evening in 1958. That was the last service at which my friend preached – he passed away in 1960.

I don't sit and brood 'beside the silent sea', as Tennyson puts it, but it does become more exciting the nearer you come to the frontier between here and hereafter. It is the privilege of a Christian to make life without Christ seem a poor thing by comparison. I once attended a funeral of a University colleague, and as we left the cemetery a colleague said: 'Well, that's the end of him.' On the morning when he was led out of his prison for his execution, the world-famed 20th century German theologian Bonhoeffer's last words were a message to his trusted English friend, the late Bishop of Chichester – 'Tell him for me this is the end, but also the beginning.'

One great difference between a Christian and a non-Christian is this blessed hope. An article under 'Centrepiece' written by Bernard Levin on 'The Defeat of Death' in the *New Statesman* affords a concluding illustration of my point. Let me quote – 'What does death mean now to us, who live by no faith, admit no unknown except the incomprehensible, recognize no immortality?' He ends a full-page article by reference to a Mr. Collis, who was commissioned to work as a labourer for the owner of a wood in Dorset, clearing and thinning it. He did it singlehanded and did it so well that the owner, when the work was accomplished, entered the 12-acre wood in his record by the name of 'Collis' Piece'. Mr. Collis wrote a book entitled *Down to Earth*, from which Levin quotes. 'Thus then do I achieve what had never occurred to me could conceivably happen, that a piece of English earth and forest would carry my name into the future'. Bernard Levin comments: 'That would do; that would do handsomely; with something like that to leave behind, I could die content.'

I was especially interested in Levin's idea and 'ideal of immortality' because not many years ago the University of Newcastle decided to name a few of the fields of the University Farm of Nafferton (12 miles west of Newcastle on the main road to Hexham and Carlisle, after previous Professors of Agriculture. So when any of my family pass by the last field on the left they salute it, for it is known as 'Pawson's Field' on the map of the farm.

I once had a day-dream about it. Two students sent to work in the field pause at the gate.

'Did he say Pawson's field? Who was Pawson anyway?'

'Dunno, what does it matter? Let's get on with the job.'

I believe that life's fulfilment is eternal fellowship with God. What is a piece of land bearing one's name worth compared to the bliss of heaven?

How I wish (which to the Christian means prayer, for prayer is desire expressed to God) that John Lennon, of Beatle fame, knew this secret, for then he would not have written, 'The thing I am afraid of is growing old. I hate that. You get old and you've missed it somehow.' It was the same with Ian Fleming, the creator of James Bond and the twelve best-sellers which sold 20 million copies, translated in 23 languages and which are still selling. His biographer wrote about 'the old age he feared and resented'.

To the Christian it is always true that the best is his abiding experience and hope, for he not only knows life more abundant over the years here, but has the promise of the life hereafter.

A long time ago, when on holiday in the west of England, at the seaside I sat on the front at sunset and watched the golden ball of fire sink slowly to the horizon. At one part it made a golden track across the ocean almost to my feet. There were dark patches within its track across the waters, but the eye could follow the route which led straight to the slowly sinking sun. It was a parable of life, for so it has been through the more than three score years of my days. Sunset and then, as we sing in John Ellerton's well known hymn, 'the dawn leads on another day' until we come at last to God's eternal day.

On January 7th, 1971, my dear partner, after fighting to the end an incurable disease with never failing courage, cheerfulness, thought for others and trust in God, went to her eternal home. This is what we sent to hundreds who wrote.

> *'We thank God for every memory of Jean's beautiful life of service here and in the Christian hope we look forward with joy to our blessed reunion in that life and love which are everlasting.'*

It was her greatest earthly hope that this book should at least be completed in typescript before her passing, and this was accomplished just the day before she went to heaven.

The then President of the Methodist Conference, the Rev. Kenneth Waights, made a most moving tribute to her fidelity to Christ and faithful service for His Church and the Kingdom of God. Amongst other words he said, 'Here is the glory, the ability through the grace of God to redeem even cancer till it becomes the medium of great courage and beauty.'

I wait, therefore, as patiently as I can until He who alone knows when I have finished the work He gave me to do here calls me to that service in which she now serves Him. One evening – never to be forgotten, six weeks before she departed this life – she asked me to face with her the fact that she would not be long with me here, and for an hour we talked of heaven.

'Never forget,' she said, 'I will be there to greet you when you come to join me, and in the meantime will love you more perfectly than I do now, for I am going to where all things are perfected.'

Every morning since her passing I have asked God to help her to help me during the day, *and she does.*

'O blest communion, fellowship divine! We feebly struggle; they in glory shine. Yet all are one in Thee, for all are Thine. Alleluia!'

Epilogue

The sun is now beginning to set on my earthly pilgrimage. On my last day at school, my old headmaster's opinion was: 'Well, Pawson, you're not brilliant but you're a slogger. If you keep it up, you'll get there.' I wonder if he would judge that I had got there'? It was a famous Queen, Mary of Scots, who said, 'In my end is my beginning', and the great poet, Keats, wrote, 'Call the world if you please "This vale of Soul-making"'. My own exciting and increasing conviction is that I am nearing the frontier of a new beginning, for I believe that, as a saint of God expressed it: 'Jesus Christ turns all our sunsets into sunrise.' I want to live as long as possible here but to be ready for the call at any moment to the life hereafter. To 'get there', I now believe, is so to live in Christ, by Christ, and for Christ that one day I shall hear Him say: 'Well done, good and faithful servant, enter thou into the joy of thy Lord', and on that day of all days, by His mercy and grace, to be able to look upon His face and not be ashamed.

APPENDIX

Our Methodist Witness

An Address delivered at the opening of the
Methodist Conference in Sheffield, July 13th,
1951, by

PROFESSOR H. CECIL PAWSON
M.B.E., M.Sc., F.R.S.E.
(*Vice-President of the Conference*)

I begin this address with a deep feeling of gratitude to God
for the privilege of membership and fellowship in the great
Methodist Church. Next to the highest honour any man can
receive, which is to belong to that company whom Christ
calls His friends, I cherish the knowledge that I belong to
the people called Methodists. I carry my 'Ticket of Membership' with me wherever I go. Continually I thank God for
my Methodist ancestry and spiritual inheritance, but even
more for that personal experience of Christ, found in our
beloved Church, which has made me a passionate lover of
Methodism and one of her sons by personal conviction.

We live in an age when belief in the supernatural is regarded by man as outmoded in the light of modern scientific
inquiry. It is also a world in which both the Christian faith
and way of life are challenged more strongly than ever by
materialistic dogma and indifference to God. Against this
background, I want to state some of the things most surely
believed by us and for which we stand, though imperfectly,
as Methodist witnesses to the Christian faith. 'A religion
which becomes a "perhaps" will not stand in the day of
battle', wrote John Buchan. In a world where so much is
uncertain, I want to affirm humbly yet confidently from my
personal assurance, the certainty and sovereignty of God,
and to testify to the reality of those free gifts of His love
which we offer in Christ to men of every colour and clime,
on either side of every man-made curtain or frontier. It is

our claim and our challenge that only as men everywhere accept these gifts can they possess the unity for which our world is in travail.

ENABLING FAITH

We witness, primarily, to the faith that enables men to become the sons of God. In one of the darkest periods of the last war, one of my students on military service abroad concluded his letter to me in these words: 'Faith is what I want. I must have faith.' It is the need of the human heart, of youth and age, far and wide, in our disillusioned, frustrated, postwar world. The nations have failed to achieve the freedoms of the Atlantic Charter, and rearmament is a ghastly revelation of their failure. Some would still have us believe that this failure is due to ignorance and stupidity. The remedy, they say, lies in scientific, humanistic education. I do not belittle the value of the education of the schools, but how much more realistic and relevant is Paul's diagnosis when he writes: 'The wish is there but not the power of doing what is right.' We err through disobedience to God, not ignorance; through the sin of a divided and unsaved heart. Men must be blind indeed, if, at this hour, they cannot see that the world needs saving, and that surely means the salvation of men and women.

'Have faith in God' is the only adequate word for a world in which faithlessness abounds. Fidelity and integrity have their ultimate source and authority in a recognition of God and a right relationship to Him. We believe in a personal saving faith in Christ, and in a personal assurance of forgiveness of sin and the gift of a new life in Him. These, and these alone, enable a man to know a right relationship to God and to his fellow men. No one will deny our major world problem is that of relationship. The world, because of science, is now a neighbourhood. Isolationism is an illusion. We know what God intended us to know, namely, our interdependence, but we are failing, and failing badly to live as good neighbours.

Science cannot solve this problem, for it has no gospel. It has brought many benefits to mankind, but it has also provided, as Bertrand Russell reminded us in a recent broadcast, 'the means of exterminating the human species and perhaps all life on this planet'. Scientists with the Christian Gospel in their hearts, and on their tongues, can do much and could do more by a stronger united witness; but every one is either adding to the problem or helping to solve it.

Our only solution lies in the Christian Good News of reconcilation through the preaching and acceptance of the saving message of Christ and His Cross. Only thus can men be born again, and through the enabling power of the Holy Spirit, by whom this change takes place, make possible God's will being done in earth even as it is done in heaven. We find this experience in Christ at the Cross. We can only truly declare it as we share the fellowship of His redemptive suffering.

It is all of God's giving and He always takes the initiative. 'For by grace are ye saved through faith and that not of yourselves; it is the gift of God.'

In this faith we say it is possible to have a world rid of the fear of war and want, a peace which is real and not just a camouflage for a cold war, a standard of righteousness for all nations, a language of love and fellowship which all may learn and understand. With men alone, it should be clear now, these things are impossible, but with God we say all things are possible. When this faith became personal to John Wesley, he was enabled to pray for his enemies. In the end, that is the only way of converting an enemy into a real friend. That is the faith by which we, and all men, can be cleansed from the guilt and power of sin, and enabled, through the continuing work of the Holy Spirit, to become the sons of God, as we are fashioned into the likeness of God's Son.

EMANCIPATING FELLOWSHIP

We witness to the offer of a fellowship which emancipates. It can set men free from the bondage and bar of colour, class and cast. 'East is East and West is West and never the twain shall meet' may seem more true now than when Kipling wrote it, but 'in Christ there is no east or west'. I know it, because I have seen men of all sorts and conditions made one in Christ. Methodists emphasize a warm-hearted fellowship which is the gift of God in Christ, created and inspired by the Holy Spirit. Our condition of Church membership is a welcome to all who desire to be saved from their sins. We believe in the Sacraments, but it is fellowship in these with our Lord and with each other which we stress. We have no barriers to intercommunion. We invite to Holy Communion, to the Lord's Table, all whom we believe He would welcome. In our Methodist class meeting or Fellowship group, we have witnessed, and still do witness, to our need of Christ, and of each other. It is the finest school I know for spiritual education, and I speak from the experience of meeting weekly for forty years. Here we learn, when first things are kept first, of the meaning of 'the priesthood of all believers', as by prayer and testimony, sharing and serving, questing and crusading, we experience an ever-widening and deepening emancipation from self, through fellowship with God and with His children. We come to know what Paul meant when he wrote, 'Who is weak and I am not weak?'

In our larger conferences, fellowship is the dominant feature and we often do our best work in these by dividing up into small groups. This rich, spiritual fellowship of our common life is one of our greatest contributions to the Church Catholic. Where it languishes, Methodism can never be at her best. We began as a society, it is still our name in the universities, and throughout Methodism we continue to hold our annual society meetings. Our organization, as with the early Christian Church evolved from the fellowship. We are not unmindful of the need for Church Order. We humbly claim to be, as a Church, Catholic, Apostolic and Reformed, but we are more concerned for that fellowship which is an expression of the freedom of God's Spirit. Fellowship, guided by the Holy Spirit, has life, flexibility and creative power. It needs organization, and we are grateful to God for our Methodist organization. Let us watch and pray that it may remain an instrument of the Spirit, a means, not an end.

As a Church, we are called at this time, so I believe, to a fuller expression towards those, both within our ranks and outside them, of this emancipating fellowship in the sharing of God's material, as well as spiritual gifts. 'One family we dwell in Him' was Charles Wesley's description of early Methodism. We are challenged to make more clear the widest and deepest implications of the Christian family spirit. The time is ripe for an adventurous and more realistic expression of Christian community living. We need to work out and live out a twentieth century witness to a redeemed society. Methodist Christians, by their inheritance and experience, have, I believe, an unparalleled opportunity to make their contribution to this witness to what Christian fellowship means in all our relationships to all men. Each for all and all for each is only fully realized when Christ is all in all. In this we have a fine incentive for missionary service; for in its world setting, it means a fellowship of all nations, living in God's world as the family of His children.

I believe in spiritual law in the natural world. Neither Malthus nor Marx but the Master of life has the last word for a world in economic confusion and strife. It is 'seek ye first the kingdom of God and His righteousness . . .' Soil erosion, malnutrition, and selfish competitive interest are the symptoms of a sin-diseased, and therefore disordered world.

As an agriculturist, I glory in Paul's vision of nature's as well as human nature's, emancipation: 'For the creation waits with eager longing for the revealing of the sons of God.' God intends this world to be a foretaste of heaven, not a hell of hate, suspicion, and bloodshed. I believe He can make the earth yield sufficient increase to feed His children and open up the channels for fairer distribution, if we are really willing to work to His plan and rule. The full sharing of God's gifts of helpful knowledge and material things would enable increased agricultural efficiency and production, and also clearer channels of distribution, resulting in the expansion in world trade. I tell my agricultural students that the only way to sanity in this mad world is for men to learn to do all to the glory of God, and so use all His gifts for the blessing of all. It is one world, and 'God hath made of one blood all nations of men to dwell on the face of the earth'. Christian fellowship is the key to sound economics.

Let us seek afresh the creative power of the Holy Spirit, in whose guidance our Methodist fellowship was born. Let us ask for that vision of heaven which He desires us to express on earth, for that fellowship in things material and spiritual which is concerned with men's bodies as well as their souls, which sacrifices that others may share, that the kingdoms of this world may become God's Kingdom. If we seek the answer through persistent prayer and dedicated thought,

'We shall not full direction need, nor miss our providential way.'

ETERNAL FREEDOM

We witness to the gift of eternal freedom, the freedom of the soul of man. Everywhere men desire freedom. Many are even willing to accept political bondage as the price of promised material freedom. The only freedom which can really meet the need of men is freedom to do God's will.

There is an essential continuity about the Christian experience which makes all who are Christ's freemen one in Him throughout the centuries. John, in his doxology of the redeemed in the Revelation, glorifies the Saviour who, to use his words, 'loosed us from our sins.' Charles Wesley, nineteen centuries later, sings of this experience:

My chains fell off, my heart was free.

When men know that experience, they lose the chains which hold the soul in bondage to sin and death. They experience the freedom which is the source of all true freedom, here and hereafter.

For in this pilgrimage through the calendar months and years, the life of time which Keats described as 'this vale of soul-making', the Bible declares 'we have no lasting city'. Only in eternal fellowship with God can man find his true home. God has so made us that all desire remains unsatisfied save in Him. The restlessness of our modern world is evidence of our neglect and need of God and also of His Spirit's continued striving with men.

We have a message to men about the greatest and most solemn fact of life, which is death. We say that the Christian interpretation of death gives meaning to life. We believe 'there is a land of pure delight' for all who in Christ accept the gift of eternal life. It is a life where suffering never invades, where death can never separate, and where 'with the morn those angel faces smile which we have loved long since and lost awhile'. We believe that those who have departed this life in this faith and fellowship belong for ever to us because they belong for ever to Christ. Every man, be he saint or sinner, has, sooner or later, to face this great question-mark of life, which is death. To the Christian it is answered in Him who is the Resurrection and the Life. All earthly hopes come to an end, but the Christian hope lights up the valley of the shadow, and leads to the land of eternal light. There in a life of purposeful activity, freed from the limitations of this mortal life, they serve Him day and night. These are they who have received the freedom of the eternal city of God.

These, then, are the gifts of God's love, which, in the Name of Christ, we offer to men everywhere, in this year of our Lord, 1951; Faith, Fellowship, and Freedom as the way to every life's fulfilment. The alternatives, never more clear than today, are fear, frustration, and futility, with no hope beyond the tale of three score years and ten.

EARNEST EVANGELISM

Never was there a greater need for more Christians and more Christ-like Christians to make the offer of these gifts more clearly and widely known. Is it possible that, knowing these things and possessing these gifts ourselves, we can be any other than earnest evangelists? It is a wise direction that on the agenda of our leaders meetings, quarterly meetings, and synods appears the subject 'Conversation on the Work of God,' but how many of us bear testimony to God in our daily conversation? Personal testimony by lip and by life in daily occupation was mighty contribution to the spread of early Methodism. We sing: 'O for a thousand tongues to sing my great Redeemer's praise', but we are not very good, in these days, at using the tongue we possess in commending our Saviour in our daily contacts. Both by our words and lives we can do more to preach not ourselves but Christ. I recall that fine word said of Scott Holland: 'His whole life is a rendering of Christianity into language we can understand.'

How greatly we need, along with fellow Christians in all the Churches, to return to God that, through repentance and faith, we may be revitalized and then do works meet for repentance. We need a stronger belief in our beliefs. Let us say again and again, 'I'll take the gifts He hath bestowed and humbly ask for more,' until we know an irresistible urge to make them known.

The secret of this desire to bring the knowledge of God's gifts to those who do not share them is a passionate love for our Lord. By this shall all men know that we witness to a love more revolutionary and dynamic than hate. Through a greater love of Christ and for each other, I believe, we should find the way to a more united witness of the whole Christian Church. I do not want uniformity, but I yearn for a clearer witness to the unity of all Christians. There is, I am told, much apathy on this question among the rank and file of our churches, but I believe that if our leaders would give a stronger lead, they would be surprised at the response.

We can all do our part in making this more effective witness possible by beginning with ourselves and God, on our knees in personal and intercessory prayer. Our greatest need as a Church is a quickening and deepening of our spiritual life – all other needs are secondary to this one. I long to see, throughout the whole of Methodism, more groups of praying people, seeking earnestly for this vital blessing. To see again the vision of the Crucified Saviour and the desperately needy world for which He died, which is crucifying Him afresh, would, I believe, make possible more fellowship through evangelism and more evangelism through fellowship. Praise God for many signs of this revival of the sense of the vital function and mission of the Church and of the results which follow. 'O that all might catch the flame, all partake the glorious bliss.' This is the way to recover the sense of urgency in our witness which surely is the explanation, in large measure, of the success in spreading the Gospel in the early Christian Church, as was the case in early Methodism.

Then let us recall the nation to God, back to the Bible, to Sunday worship, and to the building of Christian homes as well as more houses. As Christian patriots let us fight with clean hands the evils of drink, gambling, and immorality in all its forms, ever remembering the Christian principle to 'Overcome evil with good.' Let us ask God to make this nation, situated as it is between what are called the two Great Powers, a place of spiritual leadership, a centre from which light and truth may go forth for the healing of the nations. In an age of slogans, I commend to you a vow, a free translation of Isaiah's great promise which I have made in my own soul: 'For Methodism's sake will I not hold my peace and for Great Britain's sake I will not rest until her righteousness shines forth as the brightness of a new day and her saving energies as a blazing torch.' And this, I hasten to add, to be a means only towards the end that God may be glorified in His whole Church and throughout the wide world.

Which leads me to say this word to that glorious company we call Methodist Youth, for whom I have always had a special place in my heart. To them I would say, make these great gifts of the Christian faith your own – they are yours if you really ask for them. Learn to pray and keep on praying. Prepare your witness and ask the Holy Spirit in this to inspire, equip, and empower, and then to guide you in saying the right word, at the right time, to the right person. Spend and be spent in that service which is perfect freedom. Study to find new ways of declaring the timeless message to our age. Never be satisfied at any time with less than Christ's best for you, which is the way to holiness, to that goodness and wholeness of life which is our finest argument for the Christian faith. Give yourself, with complete abandonment, to the greatest Leader and to the finest cause in all the world. Go forth believing in the Holy Spirit's limitless power, and you will be mighty before God to the pulling down of the strongholds of evil and to the bringing in of that Kingdom which is the purpose of God and the destiny of redeemed humanity.

These are the days for Christians to take the lead, to win great victories for Christ, to prove that our faith in God not only endures but can overcome the world of evil. With this faith and witness we may be called, as were some of the early Christians, and some in other lands today, to suffer persecution and martyrdom, not accepting deliverance through compromise. We do not know what the future has in store for those whose faith in Christ expresses itself in faithfulness.

What we do know is that God always has the last word, that His love has triumphed and will triumph over the worst that men can do, and that His Kingdom is an everlasting Kingdom. To serve the present age in that faith is our glorious privilege. Wesley's vision was large enough to conceive of the world as his parish. Ours is the challenge, as we lift high the Cross of Christ, to witness to the truth that God, and God alone, can save a lost world.